71° North 17° East

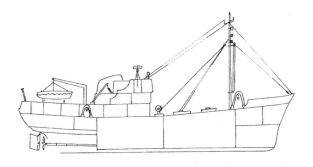

MALCOLM R. ALDRIDGE

SERENDIPITY

First published in 2003 by
Serendipity
Suite 530
37 Store Street
Bloomsbury
London

British Library Cataloguing-in-Publication data
A Catalogue record for this book is available from the British Library

ISBN 1–84394–064–7

Printed and bound by Alden Group, Oxford

To the skipper
and the crew
of the *Oratava*

Contents

Acknowledgements

ABUNDA FISHING COMPANY; Boston Deep Sea Fisheries; Grimsby Exchange and Hull Exchange; Mr and Mrs Holroyd; Miss C Holroyd; Grimsby and Lowestoft Navigation Schools; Mr R.C.E. Lander and Lloyds of London; Mr D. Page; Mr W.D. Smith; Mr R. Symonds; Mr Vickers; Miss G. Williams; Mr George Goldsmith Carter for extracts from *Red Charger* and *Looming Lights*; Mr Roy Perrot, BA (Oxon.) for extracts from *Discovering Deep Sea Fishing*; Mr Mark Stopper and Mr Ray Maltby for extracts from Boston Deep Sea Fisheries; Great Yarmouth and Lowestoft Employment Offices; Local Authorities at Grimsby and Lowestoft; Probation Offices at Grimsby and Lowestoft; Lowestoft Fishing Vessel Owners Association; Putford Marine – Lowestoft; Mr Richard Barratt; Austin Mitchell and Anne Tate – The Rise and Fall of Deep Water Trawling. Many thanks to the *Daily Express* for allowing reproduction of the article on page 138; Attempts have been made in all cases to find the copyright holders of the photographs in this book.

PHOTOGRAPHIC ACKNOWLEDGEMENT

I wish to thank the *Grimsby Evening Telegraph* for their photograph of 'The Cod End Aboard' and Innes Photographers of Hessle for their photograph of the *St Christopher*, H. 88.

Introduction

I WENT TO TEACHER-TRAINING college to study Physical Education at the age of twenty-four. It soon became apparent to the lecturers and myself that I was sadly lacking in certain aspects of the subject. I was going to have to try really hard with the two special studies required, especially the physical education thesis.

It was while we were studying dietary and calorific requirements for various sports and different types of work, e. g.: The 1960s housewife needed 4,000 calories, (although she never got it!) the same as a labourer on a 60s building site, that the question arose: 'Which type of work is the most physically demanding?' We pinned it down to fishing and mining, but could not decide which occupation was the harder.

Later, I began to think about a comparative study to find out which job was the harder, physically. I could have researched the study from books, but what if I actually observed the work? I finally decided to concentrate on fishing and try to get a trip on a long range Arctic trawler.

The college approved my plan and gave me all the help they could. The head of the PE department suggested that I concentrated my study on the fifteen-year old apprentice, a crew member on most trawlers, and that I should carry out pulse and blood pressure tests on him, after prolonged periods of work. After the trip we could work out a physical training programme for apprentices at the pre-sea training colleges. He need not have bothered. It was a different world out there.

Obtaining permission for a trip on a Distant-Water Hull or Grimsby Trawler proved more difficult than I, or my lecturers at college had imagined. I wish I had kept the letters from several large Hull and Grimsby trawler companies which refused me a voyage when I explained what I wanted to do. It soon became apparent that some of them believed my request was the start of some sort of official enquiry. There would be an official enquiry into many aspects of distant water trawling two years later with the losses of the *Ross Cleveland, Kingston Peridot* and *St Romanus*, within the space of ten days, in January 1968, due to ice top-hamper. I can clearly remember what Northern Trawlers of Hull and Grimsby said in their reply to my request: 'due to difficulties in manning our vessels, we are having to recruit as far as Manchester, and we feel that a study such as yours would be detrimental to this recruitment.'

For a time it looked as if I would have to give up the idea of an Arctic trawling voyage, but then help came from an unexpected quarter. A fellow student at college, Christine Holroyd, heard of my difficulties and came to see me. She told me that her father was a Grimsby bank manager and that he could probably help me. He did. He guided me to the Grimsby exchange where they signed on trawler crews, and I was also very grateful for the Holroyd family's kindness and hospitality while I was waiting for a ship.

At the Grimsby exchange the Manager and Recruiting Officer promised to do their best to find me a trawler sailing during my Easter vacation, 1966. The Recruiting Officer did find me a ship, but I had to promise not to publish any of my findings. He reiterated what Northern Trawlers had said. He realised that conditions, especially in the northern winter were bad on the trawlers, and he felt genuinely sorry for the men, especially the boys, but if the kind of information he knew that I would be bringing home was published, it would be damaging to the industry.

Having been turned down by all the large Hull and Grimsby trawling companies, I finally signed on at the smallest company in Grimsby, The Abunda Trawling Company, a subsidiary of Boston Deep-Sea Fisheries, a skippers' co-operative, which owned only three ships, the

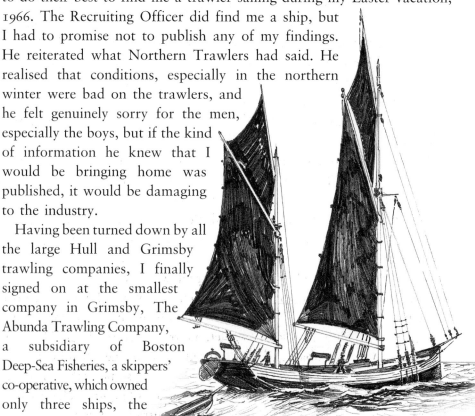

Abunda, *Bel-gorm* and *Oratava*. The skippers were all part owners of their ships, and Skipper James Nunn of the MT *Oratava*, who had two sons at college himself agreed to take me, with the following provisos: It was to be an observation trip only; there would be no time for tests on the apprentice and again I had to promise not to publish any of my findings.

When I returned, the college was very keen to get my findings published, but I had given my word, twice, and I had come to admire and respect the skipper and crew of the *Oratava*.

And so, the years passed away; some good, some bad, and I kept my journal in a safe place, along with an old canvas sea bag. Last summer, during one of my many house moves over the years, the journal surfaced again. One of my relatives read it and urged me to get it published. Now that I am semi-retired I have at last had the time to put together this book.

The surprising thing is, that as I have gone through the log of the voyage, I have found that I can remember it as clearly as if it had happened yesterday, instead of a third of a century ago. I guess it's not the sort of thing you forget, because what I saw was a life which at times was so savagely uncompromising that it had to be seen and experienced to be believed.

Historical

THE WORST ASPECT of the Industrial Revolution was the exploitation and cruel treatment of women and orphaned and abandoned children. The parish in which they were born used to apprentice them to any master who was willing to employ them and pay for their keep. Large numbers were sent to the factories and mines and others became 'climbing boys' for sweeps. Lads who lived in the coastal towns and villages were an obvious target for first the Royal Navy,[1] the Mercantile Marine,[2] or with the rapid growth of the fishing industry in the 1830s, the fishing smacks. If life is hard for a fifteen year old decky-learner[3] aboard a modern fishing vessel, it was even harder for an eleven year old bound apprentice on a sailing smack.

The main job of the apprentice was to cook for the crew. (A full-time occupation aboard a trawler today). He also saw that all tools etc., reef lacings, fenders and other small stuff were in their proper places and ready for use. He learnt to braid and mend a net, steer the ship and coil the warp when the trawl was being hauled. He was responsible for clearing from the deck the rubbish which was brought up from the sea-bed by the trawl net. With the help of the deckhand he trimmed and kept in their proper places all lights, flares, foghorn, spare pump gear and bell. Last, but not least, he obeyed all lawful commands, although how a boy of eleven to thirteen was to know whether they were lawful or not, is not stated. But he would have had short shrift if he did not jump to it when an order was given.[4]

During the nineteenth century the smacks fished the North Sea under the 'fleeting system',[5] remaining at sea for six to seven weeks. The larger smacks sailed on fourteen-week voyages to Iceland and even further north. Besides having to contend with the usual rigours of shipboard life, the long hours and hard work, the children had to face the Arctic weather conditions.

Often soaked to the skin and working knee deep in freezing water as the smack rolled in violent weather, the crews suffered from frost bite, sea boils, ulcers and laceration of the hands, which were cut almost to the bone by salt water cracks. Scurvy was also a constant menace because of the lack of fresh vegetables.[6]

By some extraordinary looseness in the drafting of the Merchant Shipping Act of 1854, there was no obligation on a skipper to report a death at sea unless the vessel was damaged as well. While illiterate men shipping in deep-sea sailing ships had to have the articles they signed explained to them by Board of Trade officials, there was nothing said about apprenticeship, especially applicable to fishing boats. There was no limit of age, nor was it imperative for a parent, guardian or any person to be a party to the indentures. Cases continued to occur where lads of eleven bound themselves for periods of up to ten years to unscrupulous individuals without realising what they were doing.[7]

From accounts given by men who served aboard the smacks there was much ill treatment of apprentices by skippers and mates.

Hideous cruelty was sometimes a definite reality when unfortunate boys could be dragged from the nearest workhouse to sea, starvelings who had neither kith nor kin to care if they were beaten, tortured or even killed.

One skipper held his apprentice's hand in a pan of boiling fat for some slight fault, whilst another madman towed his apprentice astern in the cod-end (the closed end of a trawl net) of the trawl until he died.[8]

Mr C. Alp, who was apprenticed to a smack in 1894, aged thirteen, confirmed the former incident.

One man as skipper was watching a boy frying the breakfast fish, looking through a hatchway. The boy took it into his head to try a bit of fish and the skipper went in and put his hand in the boiling fat. The lad was in that much pain that he jumped overboard and was lost. The skipper got time in jail for it, but there were a lot of such things done in those days that did not come to light. The skippers and mates were very cruel to the boys, but not all of them, there were some good ones and a lot of bad ones. I think I got more good hidings than good dinners when I was an apprentice.[9]

The following statistics will give an indication of the life led by apprentices:

Between 1868 to 1877, 4,277 lads were bound apprentices at Grimsby, and between 1875 and 1877, 569 boys were sent to prison for desertion. One boy was convicted no less than twenty-six times, stating openly that he preferred prison to the rope's end. Sentences ranged from fourteen days to one month.[10]

Things were brought to a head when two murders on Hull smacks drew public attention to the seriousness of conditions on the vessels.

In 1882 Osmand Brand, skipper and owner of the *Rising Sun* was convicted and hanged for the murder of Henry Papper, aged 14, at sea. The mate, who was also implicated, went to prison and later fled the country.

In the same year the mate of the smack *Gleaner* was hanged for the murder of Peter Hoye, aged 16. Then the skipper, mate and third hand of the *Achievement* of Grimsby were convicted for 'cruel, debasing and disgusting treatment' of two lads.

These incidents, added to certain letters received by the Board of Trade concerning lads being apprenticed without their parents' knowledge, led to the appointment of a Commission of Enquiry. Subsequent Acts of Parliament provided that no boy under thirteen could be bound apprentice and no one under sixteen could be taken to sea in a vessel of 25 tons or more, to serve in any capacity, unless bound by an indenture.[11]

The conditions brought about the extinction of apprenticeship in most of the fishing ports, except at Ramsgate where it continued until 1914, and at Fleetwood where a form of indentured apprenticeship continued until the outbreak of the Second World War.

Robert Nash, a Fleetwood trawler skipper, first went to sea on a steam trawler in 1931, aged 14.

When I was apprenticed my father signed a four year indenture. You had to word hard as an apprentice in those days and a clout or a kick from the old man was all in good order, for it made you tough and it taught you endurance. That is one of the main things you need if you want to be a trawlerman, especially in Arctic waters.

My first skipper was a very tough old Dane. I was stupid enough to cheek him one day and he beat me up. He broke my nose and nearly crushed my ribs.[12]

Despite the conditions at sea the apprentices were in some ways more fortunate than those who worked in other trades. Compare the young mill hand or sweep's boy trudging wearily home in ragged clothes to his meagre meal in the slums, with this account of the youthful Aldeburgh 'cod-bangers'[13] as their ships sailed into Harwich harbour:

They would stand on deck dressed in velveteen trousers, high heeled boots, hand-knitted jerseys, pilot jackets and silk neckerchiefs, peaked caps and small gold rings in their ears. Once ashore they would swagger down the main streets of the coastal towns with thirteen or fourteen weeks accumulated pay in their pockets. They drank, fought and made love in true sailor tradition.[14]

There were possibilities for a youth, taken from the workhouse at eleven years of age, to become a skipper at nineteen, indeed, some went on to become part-owners and eventually had a small fleet of their own. Could any mill hand see a similar reward for his labours, and how many agricultural workers could aspire to own a farm?

Thus there were compensations for the hard life for the lucky ones. For the remainder, if the hurrying waters did not claim their toll, there might be little to show for all the toil and hardship.[15]

The 'hurrying waters' certainly claimed their toll. Smack losses were appalling throughout the nineteenth century.

In one great gale in 1883, eight Grimsby smacks and twenty-seven Hull smacks were lost with all hands.[16]

In the five years 1884 to 1888, 1,328 men were lost. In 1890, 116 fisherman went missing in smacks never heard of again. In the thirty-four years between 1879 to 1913, 1,066 vessels were lost, and in over 80 per cent of these smacks, all hands were lost.[17]

Notes

1. cf. *Peter Grimes*.
2. cf. *Two Years Before the Mast*, RAH. Dana.
3. 'Decky-learner': the term applied to a boy before he becomes a competent deckhand on a modern trawler.
4. *Sailing Trawlers*, Edgar J. March MSNR (Percival Marshall & Co Ltd., 1953).
5. The smacks fished in a fleet. The catch was sent in fast cutters.
6. *Sailing Trawlers*, Edgar J. March MSNR (Percival Marshall & Co Ltd., 1953).

7. *Sailing Trawlers*, Edgar J. March MSNR (Percival Marshall & Co Ltd., 1953).

8. *Red Charger*, George Goldsmith Carter (Constable & Co Ltd., 1950).

9. *Sailing Trawlers*, Edgar J. March MSNR (Percival Marshall & Co. Ltd., 1953).

10. *Sailing Trawlers*, Edgar J. March MSNR (Percival Marshall & Co. Ltd., 1953).

11. *Sailing Trawlers*, Edgar J. March MSNR (Percival Marshall & Co Ltd., 1953).

12. *Red Charger*, George Goldsmith Carter (Constable & Co Ltd., 1950).

13. Cod were kept alive in a large well between decks, and killed by a blow from a stick when required, on Aldeburgh Smacks.

14. *Looming Lights*, George Goldsmith Carter (Trinity Press, 1945).

15. *Sailing Trawlers*, Edgar J March MSNR (Percival Marshall & Co Ltd., 1953).

16. *Discovering Deep-Sea Fishing*, Roy Perrott BA (Oxon.) (Hazell Watson & Viney Ltd., for the University of London Press Ltd., Copyright 1958).

17. *Sailing Trawlers*, Edgar J. March MSNR (Percival Marshall & Co Ltd., 1953).

Geographical and Meteorological

WHERE A DISTANT-WATER trawler could fish was limited during the winter by pack-ice and the edge of the polar ice cap. The main cycle of fishing was to work the grounds off north Norway from January to February, from there to the Icelandic grounds until the end of June then further north to Jan Mayen Island, Bear Island, Spitzbergen and Noraya Zemlya, and west to Greenland until October; from Bear Island to the White Sea off North Russia up to January and then back to Norway. However, a trawler skipper could take his vessel where he thought fit, and many preferred to fish as far north as the ice would allow, in winter and summer. An experienced man would not hesitate to take his ship through this pack-ice near the ice barrier if there were fish about but vessels were caught and crushed in the ice circles.[1]

Another danger in sailing too close to the ice cap was that of black frost and black ice. Frozen vapour blown off the ice could envelop a

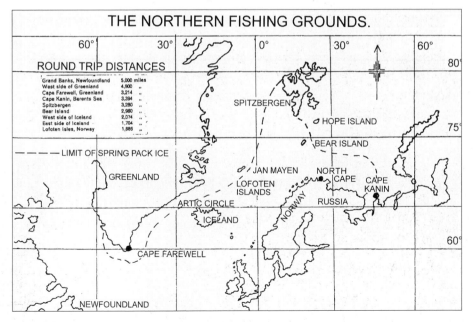

THE NORTHERN FISHING GROUNDS.

ROUND TRIP DISTANCES

Grand Banks, Newfoundland	5,000 miles
West side of Greenland	4,900 „
Cape Farewell, Greenland	3,214 „
Cape Kanin, Barents Sea	3,394 „
Spitzbergen	3,280 „
Bear Island	2,980 „
West side of Iceland	2,074 „
East side of Iceland	1,704 „
Lofoten Isles, Norway	1,886 „

— — — — LIMIT OF SPRING PACK ICE

Navigating through 'Brash' Ice, (source: unknown).

ship as quickly as ordinary fog patches. At once ice begins to form all over the ship. Trawlermen stated that you could actually watch the ice grow on the rigging. Then the ship had to sail south at full speed, while all hands turned out to chop away the ice with axes and steam hoses until the ship was clear of the dangerous vapour.[2]

During the winter, between the autumnal and spring equinoxes, the cold gradually becomes more intense and there is no daylight in late December and January. Off the north cost of Russia, the temperature can drop to −32°F and even lower. A man coming off duty will crack the enamel on his teeth if he immediately drinks a mug of hot tea, and on deck, flesh will burn and tear if a metallic object is grasped by an ungloved hand.

'I have been in places off the Murmansk Coast where the fishing was good, but which you had to leave because the men simply could not work in the cold. It was so cold that spray would immediately turn to ice, and however much the men wrapped up their faces, their breath would still turn to ice.'[3]

The other natural danger that Arctic trawlermen faced was from the wind and the sea.

'It wasn't just blowing hard, the fucking wind was screaming at us, just screaming at us. We stuck it for five days, then the skipper took us into Isafjord.[4]

'The skipper could see we couldn't take any more and brought us under the shelter of the land at Breydafjord. Along comes that Icelandic Gunboat *Thor*. They wanted to board us, reckoned we'd been fishing inside the limit. The skipper just looked at them. "The mood my men are in, you might not get off again in one piece".'[5]

Distant water trawlers were probably the finest sea boats of their size that were in existence, but a 700–800 ton, 160ft long vessel was small compared with the huge seas that Force 10 to 12 winds blow up. Many vessels foundered and sank without a trace on Arctic voyages.

One of the lucky ones was the Hull trawler *Arctic Ranger*. This trawler was struck and almost sunk by a huge wave, 140 miles south of Bear Island in January 1957, which just roared out of the Arctic darkness over the ship. *Arctic Ranger* was spun 180° off her course by the force of the impact, the lifeboat and liferafts were torn off the boat deck and lost, the after companionway stove in, safety rails bent and twisted and the ship sustained other damage. But she came up and righted herself.

Other trawlers were not so fortunate. Between 1945 and 1974, one hundred and seventy-two trawlers of over 100 tons gross, were lost at sea.[6] That is an average of five or six ships a year, pretty appalling statistics.

Notes

1. When Convoy [PQ] 17 scattered on a Russian Convoy in July 1942, the trawler *Lord Middleton* led two freighters to safety along the edge of the ice cap, through thin ice, where no U-boats dared to go.

2. A Fleetwood trawlerman informed me that he and the crew of one trawler he was on spent fifty-two hours chopping ice away before they were clear of the vapour.

3. Skipper Tom Small of Grimsby. *The Illustrated London News*, 22 January 1966.

4. Bosun – *Nottingham Forest*.

5. Deckhand – *Northern Isles*.

6. From Lloyds Register.

The Men

A T THE TIME I made the voyage if a boy wanted to go to sea on a trawler before he was sixteen-and-a-half years old he first of all had to spend six weeks at a Trawler Navigation School at a Technical College at one of the chief fishing ports such as Aberdeen, Fleetwood, Grimsby, Hull, Lowestoft or Milford Haven. (Quite a few boys managed to side-step both the age limit and the Navigation Schools!)

At the school he learnt to steer a ship, box a compass and other rudiments of navigation. He learnt how radar works and how to use navigational aids. He was taught how to mend nets and fill net needles with twine, and a certain amount of rope splicing. He was toughened physically by rowing a heavy whaler and sailing a ship's lifeboat. If he could not swim, the school tried to ensure that he could before going to sea.

While he was at the school he was paid £4 per week maintenance money and was told exactly what to expect in the way of working hours and conditions on board a trawler. However, he could not gain a true picture until he actually experienced the life at sea – the bad weather, seasickness, homesickness, the stink of fish and diesel oil throughout the ship, the stale smell of seaweed and unwashed bodies in the sleeping berths, and the total lack of privacy. Only one in ten of the apprentices leaving the Hull and Grimsby Navigation Schools did more than one trip and four out of ten at Lowestoft.[1]

In October 1967, the British Trawling Industry began formal training trips in the North Sea, taking ten trainees at a time on the specially converted Ross Mallard, for ten-day voyages. The first three or four days were spent getting the trainees used to the ship and finding their sea legs. After that the vessel carried out normal fishing activities with the boys working under close instruction. At the end of the trip those trainees who had passed in proficiency received a certificate. These training trips were a great success. All the trainees who reached the required standard of proficiency continued trawling after their first working trips.

When a boy sailed on his first trip, he was supplied with the following:

- 1 set of oilskins and sou'wester.
- 1 set of seaboots (1 size too large).[2]
- 1 gutting knife.
- 3 pairs gutting gloves.

He had to pay for these week by week to the company he sailed with, out of his wages, which were £6 a week, £3 in the £1,000 on the catch and a share of the money from the cod-liver oil. He also needed warm sweaters, underclothing, duffel trousers, plenty of socks and at least two pairs of thick seaboot stockings. He needed a woollen hat or balaclava helmet, and was advised to take a supply of barley sugar sweets and fresh fruit. The former for seasickness and the latter to keep his bowels open when he could begin to eat.

After several trips, and if the skipper considered him competent, he became a full deckhand, (this was possible while a boy was still fifteen years of age) at £13 per week and £6 in the £1,000 on the catch, plus the cod-liver oil money.

When he had put in four years sea time, he could return to the Navigation School to study for his Bosun's (or Third Hand's) ticket. He had to pass an examination on navigation, rule of the road, lights at sea, and rope and wire splicing. He also needed to know how to control men and needed plenty of ability as a trawlerman. Having passed the examination he then had to wait for a vacancy as bosun aboard a vessel. He received the same weekly wage but got £10 in the £1,000 on the catch.

Two years later he could sit for his mate's ticket which took about three months study ashore. When he obtained a berth as mate he no longer received wages but got seven and a half per cent of the catch after the vessel's expenses had been paid each trip. After serving as mate for a year and having gained confidence he could then sit for his skipper's[3] ticket. This final examination passed, he still had to sail as a mate until there was a vacancy for a skipper and some trawler owner gave him his first chance.

A trawler skipper needed to be good at his job both as a fisherman and a seaman, and he needed to be lucky too. No one could say for certain where the fish would be, but most trawler owners thought twice before giving a vessel to an unlucky skipper. There was a rota of men with skipper's tickets waiting for ships, and if a skipper made three consecutive voyages with a run of bad luck he usually got the sack and had to sail again as a mate for a period of time.

The lucky ones did make a lot of money. In 1966 amongst the more fortunate Hull and Grimsby skippers, there were seven aged 22 and 23, earning £10,000–£12,000 a year. All seven were the sons of trawler skippers.

Notes

1. Statistics from the Hull and Grimsby Exchanges and the Lowestoft Navigation School.
2. In order that they could be easily kicked off if the owner fell overboard.
3. Trawler captains were always referred to as 'skippers'.

The Ships

BRITISH DISTANT-WATER TRAWLERS which fished from the side were roughly divided into two classes:

1. Large or Distant for work in the North Atlantic and Arctic Oceans – Length 140–200ft. Gross tonnage 450–850. Voyages of 21–30 days. 1,000–2,000 [hp] 12–19 knots. Hold capacity 130–286 tons of fish.

2. Medium or Middle for work off Iceland, the Faroes and Rockall. Length 120–140ft. Gross tonnage 190–450. Voyages of 13–17 days. 700–950 [hp] 10–12 knots. Hold capacity 62–112 tons of fish.

The 1960s saw the advent of the stern-fishing trawlers which brought in their catches over a stern slipway. There were different categories of this type of vessel ranging up to the large factory ships, an example of which was the 2,600 ton *Fairtry*. She was 245ft long with a lower deck containing machinery for processing the fish and freezing them into solid blocks of ice. This vessel stayed at sea for three months at a time, usually off Greenland and Newfoundland. One of the main advantages of this type of vessel was that the deckhands could work most of the time under cover. The factory ships did not carry apprentices due to the length of time spent at sea.

Distant-water trawlers and other classes of these vessels were designed and built with the ability to keep at sea in all weathers, and taking the strain of a heavy trawl also demanded very strong construction.

In the twenty-nine years between the end of the Second World War, and the loss of the *Gaul* in 1974, 172 trawlers of over 100 tons gross were lost at sea.

Fleetwood lost fifteen trawlers[1] in the eleven years 1936–47. The port lost fewer vessels due to enemy action in World War Two than were lost by natural causes during these years.

The statistics for trawlers lost in the Arctic during the years 1960 to 1970 are:

- 1960 1 vessel lost. 16 of the 21-man crew were saved.
- 1961 1 vessel lost with all hands.
- 1963 1 vessel lost with all hands.
- 1964 1 vessel lost with all hands.
- 1965 2 vessels lost with all hands.
- 1966 2 vessels lost. All hands saved from one ship. 12 crew dead and 13 survivors from the other.
- 1968 3 vessels lost. 1 survivor.
- 1969 1 vessel lost with all hands.[2]

Over 200 trawlermen died on those ships. It seems a high price to pay for fish and chips.

The only legislation in the United Kingdom to protect fishermen from accidents and their consequences was in the Merchant Navy Shipping Acts and Rules which required fishing vessels to carry life-saving, fire-fighting and medical stores.

The heavy machinery and the strain on it, caused by dragging a heavy trawl net and the weight of about three thousand feet of one and a half inch thick steel wire being dragged astern, made the fatal accident risk in fishing twice as high as coalmining. Between 1961–65, fatalities were 9.3 per ten thousand for British trawlermen.

The heavy winches were extremely dangerous because it was impossible to fit a guard over them. Even if a man did survive being caught in the winch, he would not have long to live because of the terrible injuries caused. Accidents of that type happened during shooting and hauling the trawl nets.

Men were crushed by the weight of the great otter boards, as they crashed up to the iron gallows when the mouth of the net broke surface. Many trawlermen lost[3] one or two fingers, nipped off between the otter boards and the side of the ship.

Others lost fingers, hands or limbs because they have fallen or stepped too close to the quivering wire warps being wound into the winch. I was constantly being told not to stand over the warps. A fifteen year old 'decky-learner' on his first trip to sea on the *Oratava*, lost the first digit of his right hand when he tripped and fell near one of the wires as the ship was hauling. His finger was so badly flayed that he had to be taken to Kirkenes, North Norway to the hospital and left there.

Although ship owners and builders paid considerable attention to the design of trawlers there were no regulations governing the height of bulwarks and the provision of rails to prevent men falling overboard.[4]

The low sides were of course necessary for hauling in the net.

There were no regulations for ensuring the stability and navigability of vessels under difficult weather conditions or in heavy seas. In the wheelhouse of every trawler was a notice stating that 'No vessel should proceed at full speed in bad visibility such as snow or fog'. But how many skippers racing home at top speed with an excellent radar system took warning of that notice?

But because so many ships were lost, 'reported missing', skippers were required to report to base every twelve hours, report to coastal stations en route, keep in touch with other trawlers whilst fishing, and report themselves to passing ships.

The *Oratava*, a 165ft, 650 ton distant-water trawler, with a speed of 13.7 knots, was commissioned in 1958 as the *St Christopher* for the St Andrews Fishing Company of Hull and was sold to the Abunda Trawling Company of Grimsby in 1962.

When I sailed on her the vessel was only eight years old, but a measure of the terrific strain the ship underwent in her 340 days at sea each year was that she had already been in dock for refits three times and was due for another in May 1966.

The *Oratava* docked at 5 a.m. on Wednesday 30 March and landed 24,000 stones of fish, after a successful trip to the north Norwegian grounds. Less than forty-eight hours later I was sailing on her for yet another of her three week voyages to the Arctic.

Notes

1. From Lloyds Register.
2. From Lloyds Register.
3. See explanatory diagrams on p.44.
4. Sides of a ship.

Prelude

North Wall – Grimsby

0130 Hours 1 April 1966

A s we approach the trawl docks the ship's runner,[1] gives me one last piece of his excellent advice. 'They'll be in a funny mood the first two or three days out. Best not to talk to 'em. If they speak to you, then you can talk to 'em. Ask the skipper or Cook if you need anything.'

We drive onto the quayside of the North Wall Dock and pass a long row of deep-sea trawlers, lying alongside each other, moored bows on to the quay. The line ends and we stop by the Distant-Water Trawler *Oratava*, which is to be my home for the next three or four weeks. The ship is ready for sea, moored starboard side to the quay, her bows pointing to the lock gates.

Now that I have finally arrived the doubts begin to crowd in.

The ship's runner bids me good luck and a safe voyage and turns round and speeds away.

There is a strong north-east wind blowing in from the sea. The wind feels freezing and I pull the collar of my duffel jacket up around my ears, and do up the top button of my shirt. I check the time. It is a quarter to two in the morning, Friday 1 April – April Fools Day. But there will be no jokes where I am going.

Time for a cigarette.

Soon I am shivering, and not just from the cold. It was very hot in the Pink Flamingo Night Club in Cleethorpes, where only an hour ago I was sitting with friends at the bar, drinking strong barley wines and trying to see further down the lovely cleavage of the dark girl in the low cut white dress sitting next to me. The 'Dutch' courage the barley wine gave me is rapidly evaporating and I'm shivering from fear as well as the cold.

Ever since yesterday morning when I went to the offices of the Abunda Fishing Company to sign on as a supernumerary member of the *Oratava*'s crew, my doubts about the voyage have been growing. It was when the clerk, who was signing me on, looked up and asked me, in a very serious voice: 'Next of kin?'

The time factor is worrying me too. We will be at sea for three weeks at least, longer if catches are poor. Then there are the dangers of ice top-hamper,[2] icebergs, growlers,[3] dangerous deck machinery, wartime mines and Russian subs.

And to me the *Oratava* does not look big enough or long enough for a Distant Water Trawler, surviving up in the furthest wastes of the Arctic Ocean. She looks more like a Middle-Water Trawler designed for fishing off south-east Iceland, the Faroes and Rockall. Her whaleback[4] looks too short and stumpy and her foredeck looks too short.

She has got the raked tripod foremast to help combat the effects of ice top-hamper, the raked bridge and funnel and the long boat deck aft. But ... time for another cigarette.

I've got a bad feeling about this voyage, despite the assurances from several different sources that the *Oratava* is a 'good sea boat' and a 'well found' ship and that the Skipper, James Nunn, is a skilled fisherman, seaman and navigator, not the sort of sailor who would take risks necessarily or unnecessarily especially in bad Arctic weather.

I could walk away now, tell them back home and at college that no fishing company would allow me to go. And that actually is the truth. It's only because I know Christine Holroyd at college, whose father is a Grimsby Bank Manager, who knows Skipper James Nunn, who has two sons at college himself, that I am allowed to go. And I had to give my word that I would not publish any of my findings.

I look at my watch – half past two.

The crew have been drifting aboard, singly or in twos and threes, in various states of intoxication for the past half hour. A few of them are so drunk they have to be helped aboard, and the 'help' is none too gentle either! Now I know exactly what the ship's runner meant when he said, 'I hope you won't mind sleeping amongst a lot of drunken men.'

I light another cigarette with some difficulty. The Zippo Storm Lighter does not seem to have been designed for Grimsby's North Wall in a gale of wind.

I look up, just in time to see a ship gliding past *Oratava*. Now that one really looks like a long range Arctic Distant Water Trawler. I can just make out the star on her funnel. It is the *Ross Renown*,[5] slowly gathering speed as she heads for the lock gates. At 200ft and a top speed of 17 knots, she is one of the largest and fastest 'sidewinders'[6] ever to sail out of Grimsby. Aboard her on his seventh trip is John Brately, whose first trip was televised on the BBC's documentary film *Decky-Learner*.

Now, if I was only on that ship ... but I'm not. I'm cold, I'm tired and I have had too much to drink. All I want at this moment is my warm bed back home, even though it is only a council house. I come to a decision: 'Right. That's it. I'm not going. I'm going home.'

I shoulder my trawlerman's canvas shirt bag[7] (well, at least I tried to look the part!) pick up my sports bag, and turn away from the *Oratava*. I take one step and nearly get knocked over by the shiny new station wagon which screeches to a halt in front of me.

The man who gets out is short with glasses, (I'm just about to ask him if he needs a new pair, when I remember the ship's runner's caution) very stockily built and very smartly dressed. He is also very sober. He nods to me as he gets out and moves swiftly to the boot. He reaches in and throws a crate of oranges out. I think this must be the captain.

I start to pussyfoot away, when his commanding but friendly and cheerful voice stops me.

'You the student? Right get your gear aboard and just give me a hand with this crate.'

'Er, yes sir.' Well, looks like I am going after all!

I follow the Skipper over the rail, and another crew member grabs the crate of oranges and follows the Skipper as he makes his way aft, rounds the after casing and steps through a hatchway. I follow and fall over the hatchway entrance[8] as I did not realise that I needed to step high over the combing.[9]

Another crew member invites me down to the main cabin where the Bosun and Deckhands sleep. Five crewmen are drinking a toast 'to the voyage'. One young very tough looking deckhand, with a hairstyle like the sixties Elvis Presley, is telling his shipmates that he is down to his last clean shirt. All the rest are ripped and bloodstained from the fights he has had in the slightly less that forty-eight hours he has spent ashore since the *Oratava* docked at 5 a.m. on Wednesday 30 March.

Although the ship was thoroughly cleaned and scrubbed on the homeward leg of the previous voyage a few days ago, the cabin smells stale and dank, a smell compounded by the odours of the cleaning fluids and disinfectant, strong tobacco smoke, unwashed feet and clothing, and a deep-sea smell like seaweed.

I'm handed a dram glass brimming with dark rum. I take a swig and immediately choke on the very strong spirit.

'Elvis', (I never did remember his name, and I was too busy trying to steer clear of him all the trip, to find out.) who had given me a friendly grin when I first climbed down into the cabin, now looks at me suspiciously:

'First trip?'

'Er, yes.'

'Where ya from?'

'Er, Yarmouth.'

'Fuckin' 'ell! A fuckin' Yaco!'[10] he snarls.

The speed (although he has had a lot to drink) with which he launches himself at me from his seat, is matched only by the speed with which the other crew members pin him down.

I just stand there petrified.

I'm advised to go up to the galley for a cup of tea. As I climb back up the companionway stairs, I can hear them admonishing Elvis.

'How many more fuckin' times have we got ter tell ya? No fuckin' fighting down 'ere!'

Then Elvis protesting, 'Either that Yaco gets off this fuckin' rust bucket or I do.'

I get a much kinder reception in the galley from the cook.

'Never mind 'im. He'll be OK when he sobers up tomorrow or the next day.'

He takes me to a two-man berth midships. In the lower bunk a crewman is snoring loudly, still fully dressed in his smart shore clothes.

'Now,' says the cook, 'this 'ere is Sonny Kelly. Skipper put him in 'ere with you. He'll show you the ropes like.'

By the look of the large bottle of spirits clutched tightly by the sleeping deckhand and the two bottles of lemonade lodged in the side of his bunk, it could well be some time before he can.

I climb up to the top bunk and put my two bags on it. That's as far as I get. The clang of the engine telegraph echoes around the ship, and the sound of the donkey engine[11] is drowned by the sound of the main engines starting up. The *Oratava* shudders, then steadies.

I quickly make my way aft and round to the starboard side of the ship. I glance at my watch. It is now four o'clock and apparently there is not much water left under the keel.

The Skipper thrusts his head out of one of the starboard side wheelhouse windows.

'Get a back spring on 'er!'

The crew manning the aft mooring lines swiftly grab a thick wire hawser.[12] We haven't even started yet, but already we are carrying out a dangerous manoeuvre. We have to warp around the bend in the dock to get the ship into deeper water.

Using main engines, the ship's winch, the fore and aft mooring lines, the quayside bollards and the warp, we slowly start to inch our way around the bend. Two of the crew are busy frightening the old nightwatchman, who has been looking after the ship, by telling him that we have a deckhand missing and he's got to come with us. There is a look of real desperation on the old man's face, until they let go of him and he manages to scramble ashore.

No doubt the mathematics and physics of this manoeuvre around the quay would make a fascinating dissertation on forces and pulling and pushing, but the fact is that if the warp breaks, it will do considerable damage to us and the *Oratava*.

We slowly heave and scrape our way around into deeper water. The warp holds.

'Let go forrard!'

Oratava's bow gently swings to port, away from the quayside. The old nightwatchman waves.

'Let go aft.'

The last mooring line is hauled in, the last link with shore is cut. The nightwatchman waves again. We slowly gather speed and pass through the lock gates. We increase speed to half-ahead, turn to starboard and increase to full speed as we enter the outward-bound channel of the Humber river.

The Skipper leans out of a wheelhouse window as the crew members who were handling the forward mooring lines, make their way aft.

'Get those two below will ya!'

It seems that no one except the Skipper has spotted the two very drunk and very unconscious crew members lying by the starboard scuppers abreast of the wheelhouse. Seawater is beginning to sweep into those scuppers and over the two men.[13]

It is now a quarter past four and there is an almost imperceptible lightening of the eastern sky ahead. We are now at full speed in the River Humber. Two deckhands are busy throwing money overboard. Later I am told that they were doing this to appease the sea god Poseidon[14] to ensure a safe voyage.

The wind is dropping, but the water becomes choppier as we head down river towards Spurn Head and the open sea. The *Oratava* is riding steadily and shooting sheets of water over the bows. Even though I am aft under the protection of the stern casing, the spray stings my face.

Water is flooding in and out of the scuppers and I keep wondering what would have happened to the two crewmen if they had still been lying there unconscious.

The crew (minus the inebriated) have finished stowing the warps and are now in the large eight man berth, drinking the beer and spirits they have brought aboard. Our fifteen-year-old 'decky-learner', Graham Quantrell, is fast asleep in his bunk. On the bridge the Skipper and Mate are working out the watches.[15] Ahead the sky is lightening and I can make out Spurn Head on the port bow.

The ship's clocks are now on GMT because of our future longitude.

Notes

1. His job is to check the trawler is fuelled, provisioned, iced and to make sure the crew are aboard.

2. See section on ice top-hamper, p.125.

3. Small sharp pieces of floating ice.

4. Top of the bow section of the ship, designed for pushing aside heavy seas hitting the bows, and to give some measure of protection for the crew working on the foredeck.

5. She is sailing out of Lowestoft now as a rig standby and rescue vessel.

6. Side fishing trawler.

7. I still have that old seabag, with the handle and drawstrings made from net twine, which one of the crew braided for me.

8. Ship's doorway.

9. High step to prevent seawater flooding into the interior of the ship.

10. Grimsby and Hull trawlermen's term for those of us unfortunate enough to have been born in Great Yarmouth.

11. This provides electrical power when the main engines are off.

12. Wire rope.

13. Or *was* he the only one to spot them? As the voyage progresses, I discover that not only do most of the crew resent me, they don't like each other much either.

14. The Skipper did warn me not to believe everything the crew told me: 'You'll be writing a James Hadley Chase novel if you're not careful.'

15. A working 'shift' at sea.

Log of the MT *Oratava*
April 1–20 1966

DAY I FRIDAY I APRIL

TIME (GMT)	GYRO COMPASS	OVERHEAD COMPASS	DISTANCE (MILES)	WIND FORCE	SEA (STATE)	POSITION
0330	012°	N × E¾E		variable 2	2	Abeam Spurn Lighthouse
						Handsteering

SPECULATION AMONGST THE CREW is that we are going to the White Sea off the coast of northern Russia. If that is our destination, we will be away for at least three weeks. If the weather is bad around Norway's North Cape, we will be steaming through the north Norwegian fjords.

Although the crew's language is of the foulest variety, I notice they never take God's name in vain – as one deckhand put it, 'Poor old God, He gets the blame for everything.' Another crew member adds: 'You don't go where we go in wintertime without believing in somethin'. Anyone who does is a fool.'

0400

Our decky-learner, fifteen-year-old Graham Quantrell, has been roused from his bunk and is sharing the wheelhouse watch with the Mate.

TIME (GMT)	GYRO COMPASS	OVERHEAD COMPASS	DISTANCE (MILES)	WIND FORCE	SEA (STATE)	POSITION
0550	012°	N × E¾E	41.2	variable 3	3	A/B Flamborough Head Distance = 18 miles

The crew are turning in, still fully dressed in their shore clothes, in various states of intoxication. The *Oratava* is beginning to pitch and roll as we steam away from the land into rougher water and I'm beginning to feel seasick. (Luckily for me last night's gale dropped away very quickly, otherwise I would be feeling very ill by now.) The heavy sickly smell of diesel fuel and fumes make me feel even more nauseous, and I quickly make my way to my bunk, where I feel a bit better lying down.

TIME (GMT)	GYRO COMPASS	OVERHEAD COMPASS	DISTANCE (MILES)	WIND FORCE	SEA (STATE)	POSITION
0700	012°	N × E¾E		SW4	4	

Wheelhouse watch relieved. Normally there would be three 'steaming' watches for this bridge duty but at the moment the Skipper and the Mate plus the decky-learner are sharing watch and watch about, four hours on, four hours off. The Chief and Second Engineers are alternating on six hour watches in the engine-room, the Radio Operator has been in the radio room since 6 a.m. and will remain on duty until midnight, (he works eighteen hours a day, every day,) and the Cook is busy cooking for those who want food. The rest of the crew are asleep.

TIME (GMT)	GYRO COMPASS	OVERHEAD COMPASS	DISTANCE (MILES)	WIND FORCE	SEA (STATE)	POSITION
1200	012°	N × E¾E	101	NW5	5	

Wheelhouse watch relieved. I have been called for dinner but even the thought of food makes me feel bad.

1500 – Decky-learner's wheelhouse watch.

TIME (GMT)	GYRO COMPASS	OVERHEAD COMPASS	DISTANCE (MILES)	WIND FORCE	SEA (STATE)	POSITION
1800	012°	N × E¾E	170	NW3	3	

I get up for the evening meal, but the sight and smell of the food finally brings on my seasickness. I only just make it to the ship's side and lean over retching uncontrollably into the sea.

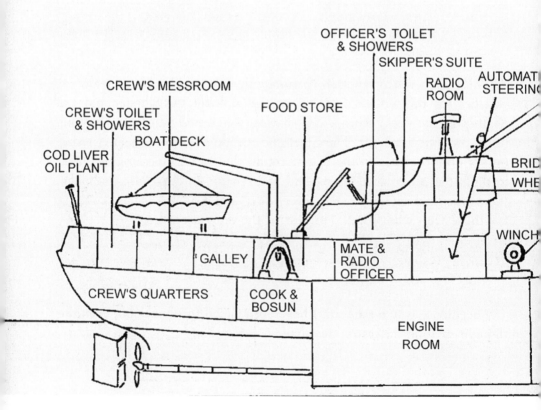

1900 – *Wheelhouse watch relieved.*

TIME (GMT)	GYRO COMPASS	OVERHEAD COMPASS	DISTANCE (MILES)	WIND FORCE	SEA (STATE)	POSITION
2300	012°	N × E¾E	227	NW2	3	

The young decky-learner is busy moaning to the Cook. Today he has worked for seven hours on wheelhouse watch, which is the easiest part of any deckhand's work aboard a trawler. The *Oratava* has automatic steering and it is just a matter of keeping a good look out for other

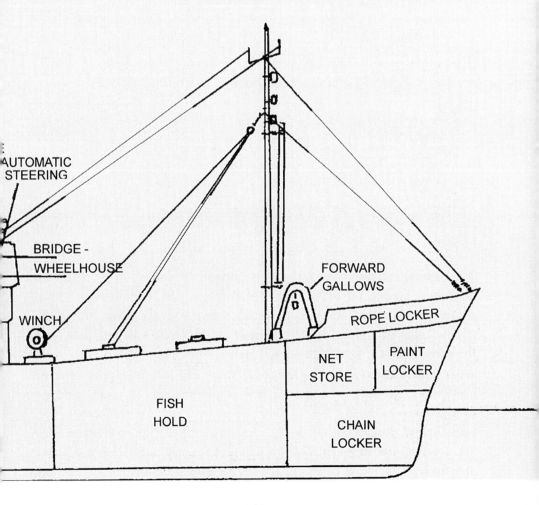

PLAN OF THE ORATAVA

AUTOMATIC STEERING

BRIDGE - WHEELHOUSE

WINCH

FORWARD GALLOWS

ROPE LOCKER

NET STORE

PAINT LOCKER

FISH HOLD

CHAIN LOCKER

ships, and using the radar screen in poor weather conditions. Usually there are three or four men on a steaming watch, but today Graham has been with the Mate. The other two members of his watch are still sleeping it off but not a word has been said to them and no attempt has been made to rouse them. Graham takes this badly. Why should he have to work[1] when others get away with it? His other duties on a steaming watch are to make the tea, and call out the next watch, also making tea for them. He is also having a gripe about this, 'Why should I have to ...' But I can't be bothered to listen to him. I go back to my bunk where I have spent most of my time today, being careful not to tread on the sleeping deckhand in the lower bunk as I haul myself up. It doesn't take me long to fall asleep again.

Notes

1. It never dawned on me until years later, that the Skipper was letting his men rest while they could.

DAY 2 SATURDAY 2 APRIL

TIME (GMT)	GYRO COMPASS	OVERHEAD COMPASS	DISTANCE (MILES)	WIND FORCE	SEA (STATE)	POSITION
0300	012°	N × E¾E	274	NNW4	4	

The Skipper and decky-learner on wheelhouse watch.

TIME (GMT)	GYRO COMPASS	OVERHEAD COMPASS	DISTANCE (MILES)	WIND FORCE	SEA (STATE)	POSITION
0700	012°	N × E¾E	320.5	NNW5	5	

Wheelhouse watch relieved for breakfast. Porridge, fried eggs and tomatoes, bread and butter, jam, marmalade, tea. I can't eat or drink anything and I can't even manage a cigarette. Every now and again I go and retch over the side into the grey choppy sea, with one arm round the after gallows to steady myself as the ship pitches and rolls in the short North Sea swells, shooting sheets of cold stinging spray over me. I can taste the salt on my lips. It is a gloomy, wintry day, cold and overcast.

I've got nothing left to bring up, just brown bile. My stomach muscles are aching from the effort of trying to bring up food that isn't there any more. I go back down below and climb into my bunk. The only sign of life below me is the sound of bottles being unscrewed as Kelly takes alternate swigs of rum and lemonade. Then he goes straight back to sleep again.

TIME (GMT)	GYRO COMPASS	OVERHEAD COMPASS	DISTANCE (MILES)	WIND FORCE	SEA (STATE)	POSITION
1200	012°	N × E¾E	379.4	NW5	5	

Dinner

Roast beef, roast potatoes, boiled potatoes, cabbage, peas and carrots. Chocolate duff and custard. Tea. Very few of the deckhands eat dinner. They are still in their bunks drinking and sleeping.

1400

The mate has succeeded in turning out four of the deckhands. They are working in the netroom, forward, under the foc'sle head, sorting and mending the spare trawl nets. The decky-learner is filling the net needles with twine for the men. He asks me to help him, but I am feeling too ill. I drift back to my bunk again.

TIME (GMT)	GYRO COMPASS	OVERHEAD COMPASS	DISTANCE (MILES)	WIND FORCE	SEA (STATE)	POSITION
1800	012°	N × E¾E	447	NNW5 to 6	5	

Tea

Ham, spam, corned beef, chips, fried egg, jelly and custard, biscuits, fresh bread (the Cook bakes a dozen loaves everyday) butter and jam. Tea.

This is the last meal of the day served aboard a trawler, but cold meat, cheese, biscuits, a couple of loaves of bread and a gallon jar of pickles or onions are left on the table and tea is left to brew on the galley stove for the night watches. Nothing is ever left by breakfast time.

Every crew member – except Kelly – has managed to turn out for some food this evening.

1830

Second sitting for tea, the decky-learner's watch. He grumbles quietly to me (nobody else bothers to listen to him). 'Why should we have to wait for second sitting? We've been working all afternoon. How come these lazy bastards get their food first? They've been turned in all day.'

I don't know and I don't care. I go and lean over the side again. It's very cold on deck now. The cloud has lifted slightly towards the western horizon and the kind of orange red sun you see in December, in more southerly latitudes, is about to set.

I go below and climb back into my bunk. I've lost track of the number of times I have done this over the past two days. If we're out for three weeks I've got another nineteen days to get through.

I watch my jacket hanging on the hook at the end of my bunk, swinging endlessly to the left and then to the right, seven seconds to port and twelve seconds as the ship rolls back to starboard. That's besides the pitching and tossing as the *Oratava* punches into the waves. I doze off again.

TIME (GMT)	GYRO COMPASS	OVERHEAD COMPASS	DISTANCE (MILES)	WIND FORCE	SEA (STATE)	POSITION
1840	A/C*020°[1]		455			

2000

One of the younger deckhands, an extremely strong and well built trawlerman called Tom, comes down and tells me I will feel better up on the bridge, where the ship's roll is less noticeable. I decide to go up. I need to get a grip on myself. I'm starting to feel dizzy from lying down too much, the lack of food and the sickness. Up in the wheelhouse another deckhand takes one look at me and goes and fetches a mug of black coffee and a few dry biscuits from the galley for me. I chew and sip and manage to keep it down.

TIME (GMT)	GYRO COMPASS	OVERHEAD COMPASS	DISTANCE (MILES)	WIND FORCE	SEA (STATE)	POSITION
2150	A/C*030°	NE × N	492.9			

2155

We pass a homeward bound trawler and one of the watch says, 'Lucky buggers. They'll soon be home.' But young Tom has a different philosophy; 'No, we're the lucky ones. They're going in to come out. We're going out to come in.' I can see his point, but we've got a hell of a long way to go and we're going to be a long time out here before we go in.

2230

The Skipper's just come through the door leading into his cabin behind the wheelhouse, to check our course, distance and position. He gives me a friendly grin and says he's glad to see that I have surfaced.

TIME (GMT)	GYRO COMPASS	OVERHEAD COMPASS	DISTANCE (MILES)	WIND FORCE	SEA (STATE)	POSITION
2300	030°	NE × N	507	variable 2	2	

The wind and sea have been dropping steadily since sunset as we close the coast of southern Norway and I am feeling better.

2400

My mentor, Sonny Kelly, has just come up to the wheelhouse to stand a watch. He doesn't say anything to the other crew members up here, and they are not talking to him.

Notes

1. *Amended or new course

DAY 3 SUNDAY 3 APRIL

TIME (GMT)	GYRO COMPASS	OVERHEAD COMPASS	DISTANCE (MILES)	WIND FORCE	SEA (STATE)	POSITION
0100	030°	NE × N	531	variable 1	1	A/B Svino-Landfall Norway – Coast 24 miles Snow Squalls
0300	030°	NE × N	554	NNE 1	1	
0700	030°	NE × N	602.1	NNE 1	1	(T°48F)

Breakfast

Fried eggs, tomatoes, bacon, toast, bread and butter, marmalade. Tea.

0730

The morning watch are sewing rawhide onto the undersides of two spare cod-ends, the closed end of the trawl net, to prevent splitting as it is dragged across the sea bed. It is heavy work dragging the nets up from the net locker and requires maximum effort from all hands including the apprentice.

During the morning, I help him to fill the net needles for the deckhands.

1100

We have just changed course to sail a mile east to the assistance of the Grimsby trawler *Northern Sun*, hove to and making smoke intermittently. Suddenly the crew are talking animatedly about 'salvage money' and a 'night in'. But as we come up under her stern, her skipper leans out of one of her wheelhouse windows, shakes his head and waves us on. The crew of the *Northern Sun* make it quite plain, by word and gesture, what they think of our proffered help. I forget to fetch my camera, the crew of the *Oratava* look very disappointed and we resume our northern passage. I run below to get my camera, but by the time I get back on deck, the *Northern Sun* is too far astern to get a decent photo. It's only a cheap camera anyway.

At this point, Kelly suddenly remembers that he is supposed to keep an eye on me and 'show me the ropes'. He introduces himself.

'My name is Sonny Kelly. I'm thirty-four years old, and I've spent more time in borstals and prisons than I have out of them. Now, the Skipper's asked me ter keep an eye on yer and show yer the ropes, like. Er, always remember, one 'and for yerself and one 'and fer the ship.' He pauses. 'Best keep to the lee side if it starts blowin'.'

Well, that's all I need. No wonder the crew, even Elvis, are wary of this man. Am I going to get robbed, or worse, in that two-man berth I share with him. Does the Skipper know he's put me in with an ex-con?

TIME (GMT)	GYRO COMPASS	OVERHEAD COMPASS	DISTANCE (MILES)	WIND FORCE	SEA (STATE)	POSITION
1200	030°	NE × N	664	NW 1	1	T°50F – bright sunshine

During the morning several of the crew have told me how lucky I am to have such spring-like weather and a calm sea. 'Usually at this time of year, we sail out in a gale of wind, fish through a gale and come home in a gale. You're a lucky bastard.'

Dinner

Roast chicken, roast and boiled potatoes, onions, vegetable soup (most of the crew use this as gravy) savoury duff, peas, carrots and cabbage. Fruit and custard. Tea.

I am amazed by the variety, quality and quantity of food on this ship. I never eat this well at home, we couldn't afford it. When I remark on this, the crew are quick to point out that this is not the case aboard all distant-water trawlers. On many the staple diet is soup, meat and potatoes – and fish, once you start fishing. On the *Oratava* it's all down to a Skipper who looks after his men and a skilled Cook who uses iron pots and pans.

Working on the deck in the fresh air has given me an appetite, but all I can manage is a chicken wing, dry biscuits and small helping of tinned fruit.

1300

The Skipper has just opened the ship's bond and we take it in turns to troop up to the wheelhouse, officers first, then the crew and last of all decky-learner and supernumerary, Graham and myself – to collect the luxuries that make life a little easier. The bond contains – cigars, cigarettes, tobacco, crates of beer (but very wisely, no spirits) sweets and chocolate, matches, soap and rather incongruously, tins of soup, baked beans and fruit, as if we don't get enough to eat already! Articles are approximately half of what they would cost ashore.

1400

On deck Graham is helping the crew to splice wire warps, a cold and boring job, (already it is colder although the sun is still shining) as he is unable to splice wire. He has to act as general dogsbody for the crew and they decide that I can assist Graham, holding cables for them and running about the ship to fetch various tools. I'm told to go to the engine room for the 'long weight (wait)'. I decide to fall for it, and the Chief Engineer grins and hands me a pile of *Dandys* and *Beanos* and motions me to sit down on a tool locker. Half-an-hour later Graham comes down and says that we have to make tea for the wheelhouse watch and the deck crew. During the afternoon we make tea twice for them. The deckhands generally drink over a gallon of tea a day, each. They say it helps to keep you going and keep out the cold.

Trawler tea or 'devil's brew' as the crew call it, is made by bringing a gallon of water to the boil, adding five tablespoons of tea, half a small tin of condensed milk, one eighth of a pound of sugar and bringing the mixture to the boil again. It is almost brick red in colour and stains the insides of the pint mugs it is served in as they are emptied. One can only surmise what it does to the insides of those who drink it!

During the afternoon, Kelly realises that we are one deckhand short and he makes sure that his vociferous complaints are loud enough to reach the bridge. The Skipper takes no notice of them, whatsoever.

'Well, he (the Skipper) could have waited one more tide ter' try and get someone.'

'Right, so we've got ter' share another man's work between us.'

'Are we gonna get paid fer the extra work?'

'How are we gonna share the money out fairly?'

'Reckon we'll 'ave ter 'ave a meetin' about this.'

'Well, d'yer reckon we are gonna get paid for the extra work then?'

The deckhands just nod and agree with Kelly. He's apparently got a reputation and defers to no one except the Skipper. Even the fearless 'Elvis' is wary of Kelly.

TIME (GMT)	GYRO COMPASS	OVERHEAD COMPASS	DISTANCE (MILES)	WIND FORCE	SEA (STATE)	POSITION
1800	030°	NE × N	736.5	NNE 1	1	T°47F

Tea

Fried liver and onions, chips, cold ham and corned beef, jelly and custard, freshly baked bread rolls. Tea.

TIME (GMT)	GYRO COMPASS	OVERHEAD COMPASS	DISTANCE (MILES)	WIND FORCE	SEA (STATE)	POSITION
1930	030°	NE × N	756	variable 1	1	

The sun is low over the western horizon. I'm up on the bridge listening to the radio and talking to the watch. Up until now the crew have either been too hungover or too fed up with the prospect of another voyage, to talk much since we left Grimsby. But now, fortified perhaps by the fresh crates of beer, they are more cheerful.

2000

Up spirits! Now that the bond has been opened, the crew receives two drams of 85 per cent proof rum each day. Graham is not allowed any of it, he's too young. Usually, the Mate or Radio Operator goes round the ship with a bottle and two dram glasses on this errand.

Looking through the starboard wheelhouse windows, I can see the full moon. It is fairly low in the sky and looks twice as big as normal. Maybe it's the clear air or some kind of optical illusion making it look bigger.

TIME (GMT)	GYRO COMPASS	OVERHEAD COMPASS	DISTANCE (MILES)	WIND FORCE	SEA (STATE)	POSITION
2300	030°	NE × N	797	North 1	1	
2330						Arctic Circle

As we listen to Simon and Garfunkel's *Sound of Silence*, (it's the first time I've heard it), the Skipper comes through from his cabin and announces: 'In case anyone's interested, we've just crossed the Arctic Circle.' Nobody is. They have crossed and recrossed it too many times before.

But I am.

Cor! I've actually crossed the Arctic Circle. Well, I feel now that I have at last achieved something in my life.

2400 – T°(F) 41°

Kelly and two of the deckhands, armed with pint mugs of tea and their tobacco tins, have just come up to stand the next watch, midnight to four, commonly known to sailors as the 'graveyard' watch, the quiet time, when your body is at its lowest ebb and you've got to stay awake.

Kelly takes in the music, the huge moon to starboard in the twilight sky and the calm sea.

'Well, all we need now is some fuckin' palm trees and dancin' girls.' He looks at me.

'You're a lucky bastard, comin' up 'ere in weather like this y'know.'

Now that he's up here, I reckon I can sleep safe and sound for a bit. As I climb into my bunk, I reflect that today hasn't been a bad sort of day after all. H'm ... only about eighteen days to go now, that's only about two and a half weeks ...

Day 4 Monday 4 April

TIME (GMT)	GYRO COMPASS	OVERHEAD COMPASS	DISTANCE (MILES)	WIND FORCE	SEA (STATE)	POSITION
0300	A/C 025°	NE × N½N	845	variable 1	1	
0430						A/B Rost-Lofoten Islands
0500	025°	NE × N½N	869.9	variable 1	1	A/B Skomverra – distance 10 miles
0700	A/C035°	NE¾N	894	ENE2	1	Coast 11 miles. T°42°F

Every day is different – I'm glad I came now.

Away to starboard is the breathtaking scenery of north Norway. The pale Arctic sun is low over the towering snow clad mountains, tingeing the peaks blood red. The sea is a deep blue, with here and there a small Norwegian seine-netter.

The extreme clarity of the air makes the land appear much closer than it really is. I judged it as two to three miles, but it shows as between ten to eleven on our radar scanner. Where the sea horizon meets the land there appears to be a sharp black line as when a film is superimposed onto another one.

Breakfast

Eggs and bacon, porridge, cornflakes, bread and butter, marmalade, jam. Tea.

We can hear the Chief Engineer having a moan to the Radio Operator, in the Officers mess room adjacent to ours, 'Skipper said to me: "Can you do some painting down the engine room this trip?" I said to 'im, "What do ya think my name is? Michael Angelo?"'

0730

It is a pleasure to work on deck this morning, with the sun becoming warmer, the sea calm and the ever-changing scenery of the snow covered, undulating peaks of the Lofoten Islands. But all the time there is the eerie moan of the wind of our passage in the rigging and aerials.

The third hand is in charge of the watch fixing the very heavy fish washer into position. It takes six of us, including Graham and myself, to manhandle the almost dead-weight metal washer up onto the supports and secure it. It takes all our strength (and I haven't got much at the moment) to lift it above our heads and onto the stand. After several attempts, when we finally do get it into position, the third hand suddenly remembers that he could have used the winch and wire warps to lift the cumbersome object.

The watch, including Graham, waste no time telling him exactly what they think of him and then burst out laughing. They could have reminded him of the winch, but deckhands will never help an officer, except in an emergency, through sheer cussedness.

TIME (GMT)	GYRO COMPASS	OVERHEAD COMPASS	DISTANCE (MILES)	WIND FORCE	SEA (STATE)	POSITION
0900			921			A/B Fuglehuk – Distance 10 miles

0930

Rigging the cod-ends of the spare nets to the main part of the spare nets. This is a highly complicated job, and the Skipper, having viewed the Bosun's performance with the fish-washer, calls out the Mate to take charge. It is tiring work as we are continually stooping, bending and kneeling in order to manhandle the nets, and the crew's language becomes more and more unprintable. Graham and I are kept very busy filling the net needles for the men. The rate at which a skilled trawlerman can 'bend' on and mend a net has to be seen to be believed. The Mate uses two yards of net twine a minute.

1030

Off our port bow is a fleet of seven, ten thousand ton refrigerated Russian cargo vessels, surrounded by several trawlers about the same size as us, transferring their catches of fish. These fleets stay at sea for six months at a time and they are slowly but surely over-fishing the Arctic Ocean. Next year a Hull Factory Trawler is being sent to explore possible grounds off the coast of West Africa, and two Grimsby trawlers are sailing for the South American coast of Patagonia.

The sight of the Russian fleet reminds one of the deckhands of an incident two years ago, on very crowded fishing grounds off south-east Iceland. The vessel he was on was trawling parallel to a Russian factory ship. Both ships were 'on fish' and neither was giving way. The fishing gear of the two trawlers became entangled and both ships had to stop; 'Well, our skipper he was jumpin' up and down and shaking his fist at the Ruskies, when this voice comes over their loudspeaker, tellin' 'im to calm down and they'd free our gear. Only, this voice was a woman's. Yeah, the Ruskies 'ad a woman skipper!'

TIME (GMT)	GYRO COMPASS	OVERHEAD COMPASS	DISTANCE (MILES)	WIND FORCE	SEA (STATE)	POSITION
1100	A/C 040°					Up Spirits
1200	040°		955	ENE2	1	T°45°F
1216			958.8			A/B Littlehoy – distance 14 miles

Dinner

Vegetable soup, (very hot, very thick, and extremely well seasoned), roast pork, roast and boiled potatoes, onion duff, peas, carrots, gravy. Jam duff and custard. Tea.

I am beginning to get my 'sea-legs' now, probably due to the fact that the sea has been calm for the past thirty-six hours. After a small breakfast this morning, I discover a hearty appetite, due to the hard work and also to the fine rarefied air, which is also breaking up a bad cold I have had for the past week. I eat my first meal on the *Oratava* and the food tastes delicious.

1330

Rigging the wire warps of the trawl around the winch, and fore and aft booms. This is highly dangerous work and we are careful to keep clear of the thick wires as they slacken and tighten very quickly. A man could easily lose a limb or have his back broken if a warp caught him. As the work proceeds, Graham and I are sent to the least dangerous position – aft.

Four years ago in 1962 aboard the Fleetwood trawler *Westella*, while they were rigging the trawl, a deckhand was caught around the thigh by a wire and carried halfway up the foremast, before the warp severed his leg. (The shocked crew did not manage to stop the winch in time). He died from injuries sustained when he hit the deck. Now the winches aboard trawlers can be stopped instantaneously by a master switch in the wheelhouse.

1430

In our own wheelhouse the Skipper is listening to reports from other trawlers. Fishing is poor at Iceland and the White Sea, and as the season is over on the Norwegian coast, he is looking worried but this could all be part of a double act. No skipper is going to let others know if he is 'on fish' and James Nunn knows a lot more than he is telling. The worried look may be there to keep the men on their toes.

TIME (GMT)	GYRO COMPASS	OVERHEAD COMPASS	DISTANCE (MILES)	WIND FORCE	SEA (STATE)	POSITION
1500			992			A/B Anda Light – Distance 8 miles

As we proceed further north the mountain ranges become higher and the peaks become more jagged and irregular.

TIME (GMT)	GYRO COMPASS	OVERHEAD COMPASS	DISTANCE (MILES)	WIND FORCE	SEA (STATE)	POSITION
1700			1015			A/B Andenes – Distance 9 miles

We are passing the town of Andenes and through the bridge binoculars I can clearly see the yellow stone houses by the entrance to Andafjord. I can also see the dome of the radar station of the DEW line, the Distant Early Warning System, a reminder that Russia is less than 300 miles to the east. High in the sky are the vapour trails of American heavy bombers on patrol.

TIME (GMT)	GYRO COMPASS	OVERHEAD COMPASS	DISTANCE (MILES)	WIND FORCE	SEA (STATE)	POSITION
1800	045°	NE	1028	E2	1	A/B Fuglhoy – Distance 11 miles T°42°F

Tea

Fried liver and onions, eggs, chips, fruit and custard, fresh rolls and bread, butter, jam, biscuits. Tea.

Over this meal, the crew tell me that we should be turning into the fjords, which run through to the White Sea around 11 o'clock tonight.

1920

But we are not going to the White Sea. The men were all surprised when the Skipper just rang down to the crew to standby. They are surprised that he is trying his luck on the Norwegian grounds as the

THE METHOD OF SIDE-TRAWLING

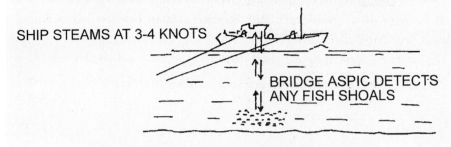

SHIP STEAMS AT 3-4 KNOTS

BRIDGE ASPIC DETECTS
ANY FISH SHOALS

THE NET IS DRAGGED ALONG THE SEA-BED
A HALF TO THREE QUARTERS OF A MILE ASTERN.

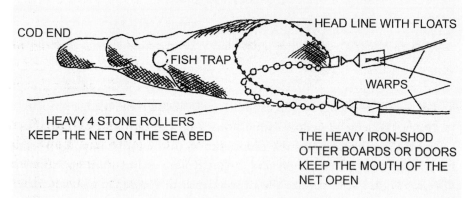

COD END

HEAD LINE WITH FLOATS

FISH TRAP

WARPS

HEAVY 4 STONE ROLLERS
KEEP THE NET ON THE SEA BED

THE HEAVY IRON-SHOD
OTTER BOARDS OR DOORS
KEEP THE MOUTH OF THE
NET OPEN

DANGEROUS DECKS

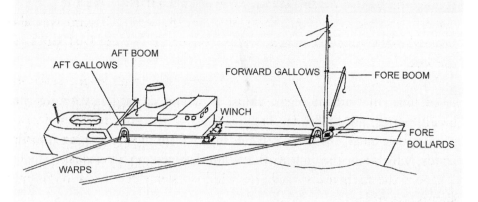

AFT BOOM

AFT GALLOWS

FORWARD GALLOWS

FORE BOOM

WINCH

FORE
BOLLARDS

WARPS

WHEN FISHING, ALL THE DECK AREAS FORWARD OF THE AFTER
GALLOWS BECOME DANGEROUS WORK AREAS

season is over. All the deck crew go below to put on warmer clothing, oilskins and seaboots. I put on tracksuit bottoms and jeans, a vest, a tee-shirt, a thin sweatshirt and a heavy fisherman's jersey which has been oiled and is very itchy.

TIME (GMT)	GYRO COMPASS	OVERHEAD COMPASS	DISTANCE (MILES)	WIND FORCE	SEA (STATE)	POSITION
1925			1045			Log Set. Fuglhoy – Distance 31 miles, bearing 140°

Ship's Log closed down while fishing.

TIME	T°F	WIND	SEA	CONDITIONS ON DECK	REMARKS
2045	40°	3	2	Cold	

Since the order came to standby we have steamed due west from the coast for three quarters of an hour and have been circling over fish shoals picked up on the echometer, which works on the same principle as the World War II Asdic, used for detecting U-boats.

The Mate, Bosun, all the deckhands, the decky-learner and myself are all on deck as we wait to shoot away the net for the first trawl. The easygoing atmosphere of this morning, in the warm sunshine, has gone.

The men are very tense as they wait, silently, 'ticklers' jammed firmly between their lips, for the order to shoot the net over the side. There are three new deckhands this trip, and everyone has to work as a team, and get it right the first time. Any mistake or mistakes can lead to serious injuries or death. This is it. This is what we came for.

I was ordered to 'get aft and stay outa' the way'. Graham was also ordered aft to help secure the warps after the trawl has been put over the side.

Everyone is warmly dressed in oilskins, and thigh-length seaboots, woolly hats or cloth caps and gutting gloves. 'Elvis' who always manages to look smart whatever he is dressed in, is wearing the latest in two piece oilskin suits, while the rest of us have the traditional long oilskin coats. Mine feels heavy and cumbersome, as do my seaboots.

One of the starboard wheelhouse windows slams down and the Skipper shouts the order.

The trawl is pushed over the side, the heavy doors, which cause so many accidents and which keep the mouth of the net open on the seabed, are 'knocked out' away from the iron 'gallows', and the winch lets out the warps. The Skipper swings the *Oratava* in a wide circle as the net sinks below the surface of the sea. When enough of the warps have been let out, the winch is stopped and the warps are secured. At three knots, we begin our first trawl. The operation of 'shooting' the net has taken twenty minutes.

As we go below, more than one of the crew remark to me, 'It's a long way to come to fish.' It is. It has taken almost four days and a thousand miles. It has cost £200 a day in fuel, food and wages to bring twenty men up here, and now we need to start earning money.

In the crew's messroom, the men drink tea, and roll cigarettes, which they store carefully in their tobacco tins. Everyone keeps their oilskins and boots on because we do not know when the Skipper will give the order to haul, and in case anything goes wrong on this first tow. On deck it is getting colder.

TIME	T°F	WIND	SEA	CONDITIONS ON DECK	REMARKS
2345	37°	3	3	Cold	

We have just hauled fifty baskets, or 300 stone of fish, and Graham has been sent to make the tea for the watch on deck before he turns in. On deck the temperature is still dropping.

Well, in theory, if we manage to catch 300 stone of fish every haul (and that's only a poor to moderate catch) and we bring the trawl in every three hours, that's 2,400 stone of fish every day, and if we manage that for the next ten days, that will be 24,000 stones of fish, which will be a good catch, and then we can go home. Good! But it never works out like that. Anyway only seventeen days to go now, with a bit of luck.

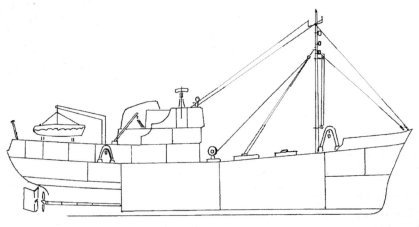

Day 5 Tuesday 5 April

TIME	T°F	WIND	SEA	CONDITIONS ON DECK	REMARKS
0645	41°	7	7	Difficult	

Every day is different.

The wind has been rising since midnight, and we are fishing in almost gale force conditions. The deck-learner has just been called for the 7 a.m. haul. He looks very tired as he drinks a mug of tea, and the pupils of his eyes are dilated.

TIME	T°F	WIND	SEA	CONDITIONS ON DECK	REMARKS
0700				Difficult	Hauling

We are hauling in the middle of a snow squall. *Oratava* is pitching and rolling in the heavy swells. The Skipper estimates the height of the wave crests as between 15ft and 20ft. The weight of the net and fish drag us over on the starboard side, and we are continually taking seas over the starboard rail which makes it difficult to keep your footing. Since our first catch at midnight last night, we have been accompanied by a horde of screaming seagulls, mollymawks and kittiwakes. As the net breaks surface, they dive on it attacking the fish. Otherwise they keep abreast of the wheelhouse, the ideal position for diving onto fish entrails as the crew gut the catch and throw the offal over the side. It is very noisy out here on the deck. Besides the cries of the seabirds, there is the noise of the sea, the wind, which is now screaming in a banshee moan through the rigging and aerials, the clatter of the winch when we are hauling and shooting, and the creak of the warps as they take the strain of the weight of the trawl and the heaving ship.

The Sequence of Hauling the Trawl

(1&2) Oratava's large and dangerous winch. Hauling the trawl takes between 15 and 20 minutes. (3) The cod end of the net breaks surface. (4) Aft otter board is hauled up to the aft gallows. (5) Aft otter board secured – view looking forward. (6) A dangerous moment as two of the crew struggle to free the forward otter board which has twisted against the ship's side. (7) When both boards reach the gallows. (8) The booms are swung out. (9)The mouth of the net is hauled up. (10) The main body of the net is winched in. (11) Part of the net is hauled in manually. (12) Finally, the cod end containing the catch is swung aboard. Photo courtesy of the Grimsby Evening Telegraph.

I'm surprised I'm not being seasick again in these almost gale force conditions, but I find the roll and pitch of the ship in these long high swells much easier to handle than the shorter choppier swells of the North Sea.

TIME	T°F	WIND	SEA	CONDITIONS ON DECK	REMARKS
0720					Shooting away
0735					Deck watch to breakfast

Breakfast

Porridge, cornflakes, fried cod, haddock and plaice fillets, bread and butter, jam, marmalade. Tea.

I have never tasted such delicious fish before. We have more or less eaten it straight from the sea, from the 0330 hours haul. It is very white in colour and just falls off the bone.

Over breakfast, Kelly glances through the hatchway to make sure the Radio Operator is through in the Officer's Messroom, and then confides to me in a very loud voice: 'Course, y'know the most hated man aboard a trawler is the Radio Operator. He sits up there in his little shack all day long, in the warm, readin' comics and 'e never gets 'is 'ands dirty, and he gets paid fer it, too!'

The other deckhands nod in agreement.

TIME	T°F	WIND	SEA	CONDITIONS ON DECK	REMARKS
0800					Gutting the 0715 catch

I'm about to go back on deck when the third hand approaches me. 'Skipper wants ta see ya. On the bridge. Now. This way.'

He leads me through the ship onto a walkway crossing over the top of the engine room. It is very noisy here as well, with the engines pounding away. Along the rails of the gantry are hanging the oilskins of the off-duty deck watch, drying before their owners go back on deck.

There are usually fourteen or fifteen seamen, including the Mate and Bosun making up the deck crew. The watches are overlapped so that the men work eighteen hours a day with six hours off. They do not object to working the eighteen-hour days. As one deckhand pointed out to me: 'There's fuck all else to do up here except work.' The one watch they all dislike is from 6 p.m. in the evening until midday next day. That one does drag. Sometimes, if catches are very heavy or if the ship starts to ice up, then their working hours will be longer, and in extreme cases they might have to go forty-eight or seventy-two hours without sleep. If the weather deteriorates to such an extent that the ship has to stop fishing, then they will get more rest.

From the engine room we go up to the bridge through the two automatic steering rooms. At the upper one I stop, fascinated by what looks like a big steel skeleton that clicks every time the ship pitches and rolls, compensating for the movement of the sea and keeping the ship on a true course. This automatic steering saves a lot of hard work at the ship's wheel in the kind of weather we are experiencing at the moment.

'Oi,' says a voice from above, 'Skipper said now!'

Up on the bridge the Skipper nods a greeting and motions me to follow him. We go through the radio room, filled with the sound of static, radio signals and voices. The Radio Operator, turning various dials also nods to me.

As I enter the Skipper's cabin, my mouth drops open in surprise. So this is one of the perks if you get to be a Skipper. I stare at the smart red carpet, the wood panelled walls and the rows of books covering one of the walls. I can also see into the en suite bathroom, which actually contains a bath. (All we've got is a shower room with one toilet, a row of urinals and two showers between about sixteen men.) But my eyes return to all the books.

'Shut the door, young man. Can't hear properly with all that racket going on.' I close the door still gazing at the books. The Skipper turns to the books.

'They're all on Christopher Columbus, finest navigator ever,' the Skipper informs me. The man's a scholar as well as a trawler captain.

'But I thought Captain Cook … '

'Aye, he was a first class navigator – and map-maker, but y'have to remember that Cook had a lot more navigational instruments. No, Columbus was the best navigator, ever.'

The Skipper opens a wooden sailor's chest at the side of the cabin and takes out some old charts.

'See these? They've been handed down from my grandfather to my father – they were both skippers as well – and then to me.' The old charts are all maps of the Arctic fishing grounds and a lot of notes have been written on them. So this is one of the secrets of James Nunn's success. 'See, they (the crew) think the season's over off this coast, but it's a matter of knowin' exactly where to go.' He taps the charts, 'and these tell me a lot.'

'Anyway, I was wonderin' if ya could help us out. I'm one deckhand short and a galley boy. Could ya give the Cook a hand aft? I'll pay ya for the work, I'll make sure you 'ave time to write yer thesis and ya can have full access to the ship's log.' Full access to the ship's log. Right.

I thank him for allowing me to come on the trip and tell him I'm more than willing to help out in any way I can.

'Thanks. OK off ya go and see the Cook now and tell 'im you'll be giving 'im a hand.'

As I open his cabin door, he asks me if I play chess, and looks very disappointed when I have to admit I can't.

I make my way back down through the automatic steering gear rooms. I find the metal skeleton, clicking away, an absolutely fascinating piece of machinery, almost human in its actions, but mindful of my new duties I go aft to the galley and report myself to the Cook. He is a very kindly, friendly little man and seems pleased that he's getting some much-needed help.

While I start to work my way through a large bucket of potatoes, peeling them for dinner, he tells me more about our Skipper.

'Sithee, me and 'im did our first trip to sea together, me as galley boy and 'im as decky-learner. When 'e got to be Skipper he asked me to go with 'im.' He lowers his voice; 'E's bin good ter me, gives me a back 'ander at the end of every trip.' I'm trying to work out why on earth the Skipper hits the Cook at the end of every trip, when I realise what he means. The Cook goes on; 'He's got a quarter share in this ship, and its not often 'e makes a bad trip. He earns so much money, 'e has to 'ave several trips off a year ter get 'is income tax back. He's buying a pub at the moment for when 'e retires like. When 'e retires, I'll retire.' The Cook pauses; 'Reckon e'll gimme a job in pub when we do go ashore.'

So, add to successful distant water trawler Skipper and scholar, successful businessman as well.

TIME	T°F	WIND	SEA	CONDITIONS ON DECK	REMARKS
1030					Hauling
1045					Shooting Away
1105					Gutting

After peeling the potatoes, carrots and swedes for dinner, the Cook asks me if I would like to clean up the crew's messroom, which is ... a mess.

With a cloth and a bucket of soapy water, I clean the table, the walls and then for good measure the leather seats. Then I help the Cook to fix the 'fiddles' across the officer's and crew's messroom tables. These are three-inch high wooden batons screwed to the table, which, in theory, will stop the plates of food, especially dishes of very hot soup from sliding across the table and cascading into the crew's laps, because at the moment the ship's motion is increasing; pitching, tossing, rolling, with every now and again an extra lurch and judder as her bows smack into a wave and her stern, including the propeller, lift clear of the water and then bang down again. You can really feel that motion where we are, aft. In fact, *Oratava* seems to be going through every motion possible, except for 'standing on her nose' as the Cook puts it.

I'm very pleased that I have not been seasick again. I'm getting the hang of bracing one leg against a roll and also the 'going with the ship' balance as the crew describe it.

TIME	T°F	WIND	SEA	CONDITIONS ON DECK	REMARKS
1155					Up Spirits

There's a kind of mystical ritual about this 'up spirits', just like the piping of the haggis. The Mate or the Radio Operator comes round the ship, very solemnly, with a large bottle of rum and two-dram glasses. Today these two glasses are held firmly down on the table while *Oratava* pitches and rolls.

Not a drop is spilt as it is poured out and then poured down throats in one gulp.

The crew are very pleased with my cleaning efforts; ('Yeh, why the fuck should we 'ave to live like pigs,' says Kelly.) insisting that I have a tot as well. So I throw it down my throat (well, I do try to look the part). The fiery liquid burns as it goes down and seems to explode in my stomach. As I gasp, one of the crew hands me a can of strong Robin

Hood Ale. This does not help at all and suddenly I feel dizzy, queasy and sick again. I rush to my 'sick' position by the starboard gallows and retch over the side. A big sea breaks inboard and I am soaking wet from my waist down. I get wet several more times before I feel well enough to go below and change.

TIME	T°F	WIND	SEA	CONDITIONS ON DECK	REMARKS
1200	41°	7	7	Difficult	

Dinner

Soup, roast beef and boiled potatoes, peas, cabbage, carrots, swedes, onion duff. Apple crumble and custard. Tea.

TIME	T°F	WIND	SEA	CONDITIONS ON DECK	REMARKS
1230					Gutting
1330					Hauling

There is a split in the trawl and we lost some of the fish this haul.

TIME	T°F	WIND	SEA	CONDITIONS ON DECK	REMARKS
1345					Mending the split net
1415					Shooting away the net
1430					Gutting
1730		6	6	Difficult	Hauling
1745					Shooting away
1800	40°	6	6	Difficult	

Tea

Cold ham and pork, chips, chicken soup, fruit and custard, bread and butter. Tea.

1930

The deck is now clear of fish. The decky-learner comes into the mess room, drinks a cup of tea and then sprawls out on one of the benches. The crew tell him off because he is still wearing his oilskins in the cabin where we eat, and then give him another telling off for making a mess after I have cleaned up.

TIME	T°F	WIND	SEA	CONDITIONS ON DECK	REMARKS
2015					Hauling
2030					Shooting away
2045					Gutting
2100	5	5		Heavy Snow Squalls but less water on the deck	
2200					Up Spirits
2300					Hauling

The 'doors' or otterboards have twisted and are jammed against the ship's side. It takes Kelly twenty minutes up on the forward gallows with a long metal wrench, aided by the searchlight as well as the deck lights to free one of the doors, and the Mate working at the after gallows to free the other. What they are doing is dangerous. They have to judge every movement of the sea, which is not easy in the dark, every movement of the ship, do the work leaning far out over the ship's side and leap back when the doors suddenly come clear and crash against the ship's side. Many trawlermen have lost fingers, hands, arms and lives because they have been unable to push back out of the way of the doors in time, doing the same job that Kelly and the Mate have just been doing.

TIME	T°F	WIND	SEA	CONDITIONS ON DECK	REMARKS
2335					Shooting away
2400	37°	5	5	Snow Squalls	

The decky-learner has just gone below for his six hours off. Despite the cold and wet conditions, he looks fit and well, apart from the shadows under his eyes. I think that sometimes the crew forgets he is only fifteen years old. Today the boy was up for eighteen hours and worked for fifteen and a half of them. The only concession he got was a two-hour towing watch in the wheelhouse with the Skipper from 1530 to 1730 this afternoon.

(1) Gutting the catch. (2) Ross Renown *seen through the* Oratava's *forward gallows. (3) 0200 hours – broad daylight. (4) A heavy sea cascades over the port side, viewed from the bridge deck.*

Day 6 Wednesday 6 April

During the past thirty-six hours, the Skipper has found that we are making the largest hauls on the western edge of the Malanger Grounds and we are now steaming back to a starting point after every three hauls.

TIME	T°F	WIND	SEA	CONDITIONS ON DECK	REMARKS
0600	34°	6	6	Wet and very cold. The wind is off the land	Gutting the 5.30 a.m. haul

The decky-learner looks very pale and tired. At first his movements are slow and laboured and the crew tell him to get a move on with his work. After about half an hour the cold wind begins to revive him and by breakfast time he is gutting at the same speed as the men.

0700 – Breakfast

Porridge, Cornflakes, fried fish, bread and butter, marmalade. Tea.

TIME	T°F	WIND	SEA	CONDITIONS ON DECK	REMARKS
0830					Hauling
0850				Snow Squalls	Gutting

We are steaming back to the trawl starting point which the Skipper has chosen. At full speed ahead through the heavy swells we take solid sheets of water over the bows, and despite the protection of the whaleback, the men stagger as the water hits them.

TIME	T°F	WIND	SEA	CONDITIONS ON DECK	REMARKS
1130					Shooting away
1200	35°	7	7	Difficult. A rising wind and sea and intermittent snow squalls	Up spirits

Dinner

Roast pork, roast and boiled potatoes, soup, gravy, peas, cabbage, and swedes. Chocolate duff and custard. Tea.

It is difficult to keep the food on your plate as the ship is rolling badly.

'Why the 'ell can't he put us on a different tack while we're eatin' our grub?' asks one of the engine room greasers.

1330

The deck is now clear of fish, and after a cup of tea, the crew kick off their sea boots and oilskins and hurriedly make for their bunks to snatch half an hour's precious sleep.

TIME	T°F	WIND	SEA	CONDITIONS ON DECK	REMARKS
1415					Crew called out for the next haul.
1430					Hauling
1445					Shooting away
1500					Gutting

1730

The deck is clear of fish again, and the crew are sprawled out in the galley and messroom drinking tea, smoking and rolling their 'ticklers'. The decky-learner is looking very tired, even through his cheeks have got a healthy glow. He does not say anything as he rolls his cigarettes. He smokes over half an ounce of tobacco a day.

Young Tom, who managed to get me out of my bunk and up to the wheelhouse on Saturday, takes me to one side.

'Look you don't 'ave to keep walkin' around the ship with yer wallet stuffed in yer back pocket all the time. It's an insult to the crew.' My hand goes instinctively to my jeans pocket. The wallet is still there. 'Ya can chuck yer wallet on yer bunk for the rest of the trip. Nobody's gonna touch it.' I mutter an apology and go down and hide my wallet in the large tin of chocolates I brought with me from home.

TIME	T°F	WIND	SEA	CONDITIONS ON DECK	REMARKS
1800	34°	7	7	Difficult	Hauling

The crew are swearing because tea will be late tonight. They do not like their routine mealtimes upset, and they are always ravenously hungry after more than four hours on deck.

TIME	T°F	WIND	SEA	CONDITIONS ON DECK	REMARKS
1820					Shooting away
1835					All square.[1]

Tea

Soup, onion duff, fried egg and chips, jelly and custard, biscuits, bread and butter, jam and marmalade. Tea.

1900

Second sitting to tea. There is a lot of arguing and squabbling going on over the food, because the first sitting helped themselves to some of the second sitting's food, while the Cook and I were serving the officers. The poor Cook gets the blame.

TIME	T°F	WIND	SEA	CONDITIONS ON DECK	REMARKS
1900				The temperature is dropping	Gutting
2100				on deck	Hauling
2115					Shooting away
2135					Gutting
2315					Hauling
2345				Very difficult conditions	Steaming back to our starting point

Up spirits. Graham looks enviously at his shipmates as they gulp down their dram of rum, and then looks disgustedly at the cup of tea in his hand. To console him, the Radio Operator gives him a can of beer. The boy will not be allowed spirits aboard ship until he is eighteen, unless he brings them aboard secretly. He has two seaboils forming near his left elbow on his forearm.

The rest of the deck crew lash their wives' and girlfriends' old stockings around their wrists before putting on their gutting gloves. This prevents most of the fish slime and sea water from running up their arms and is a preventative measure. Either no one has tipped Graham off on how to protect his wrists and forearms or he is too tired to bother.

TIME	T°F	WIND	SEA	CONDITIONS ON DECK	REMARKS
2400	30°	6	6	Snow squalls and a freezing wind	

It's going to be a hard night out there on the deck, even with dawn breaking in about an hour and a half. The wind is vicious. I am thankful to be able to go to my bunk and sleep.

Notes

1. When the trawl has been put over the side, the necessary lengths of warps paid out, and then secured and shackled, the Mate signals the Skipper with 'All square!'

DAY 7 THURSDAY 7 APRIL

0545

The 0600 hrs to midnight deckwatch are called out.

TIME	T°F	WIND	SEA	CONDITIONS ON DECK	REMARKS
0600	33°	7	7	Snow squalls	Difficult

Graham finally arrives on deck at five minutes past six after being called three times. The third time he was shaken until he did wake up. He has had less than six hours sleep and now he's got to face another eighteen hours, most of which will be spent on the rolling deck in the very cold wind.

0700 – Breakfast

Porridge, fish, bread and butter, marmalade and jam. Tea.

The boy eats his breakfast slowly, hunched up over his plate. His hair is hanging forward and going into his porridge, but he makes no attempt to brush it away. The boils on his arm are larger and inflamed this morning.

TIME	T°F	WIND	SEA	CONDITIONS ON DECK	REMARKS
0800					Gutting

It's rather a savage business gutting fish. It is also a skilled job. A fast rip and slash down the belly of the still living fish, and the entrails are thrown overboard and immediately pounced on and fought over by the screaming seabirds. The cod livers are tossed into a basket, and with a quick turn and expert flip of the wrist, the fish is thrown up into the washer. From there it travels down a chute into the fish hold where it is packed in ice. It is by no means as easy as the deckhands make it look, especially with a large cod three or more feet long and weighing several stone. The constant bending and stooping to pick up the next fish on the heaving deck is not easy either. The incoming seawater helps to clean the deck of blood, slime and excrement, but it still looks like a slaughterhouse.

TIME	T°F	WIND	SEA	CONDITIONS ON DECK	REMARKS
0830				Every time we steam at full	Hauling
0850				speed back to our starting	
1130				point, the crew have to	Shooting away
1145				contend with the sheets of	All square. Up spirits
1200	34°	7	7	water coming over the bow	
				Difficult	

Dinner

Soup, meat pie, onion duff, boiled potatoes, cabbage, peas and gravy. Rice pudding and jam. Tea.

1300

The deck is clear of fish and Graham's watch go to the wheelhouse to give the Skipper an hour in his bunk. He has averaged less than four hours sleep a day since we began fishing operations.

TIME	T°F	WIND	SEA	CONDITIONS ON DECK	REMARKS
1430					Hauling
1450					Shooting Away
1505					Gutting
1730					Hauling
1745					Shooting away
1800	34°	6	6	Easing	All square

Tea

Fried eggs, scallops, bacon, tomato, sausages, cheese, biscuits, bread and butter. Tea.

A delicious meal. Our excellent Cook is trying to cheer the men up a bit. They are fed up with the continuously bad weather and difficult conditions on deck, and there is no beer left aboard the ship.

There is growing antagonism between the decky-learner and the crew. He is far too cheeky to some of them. After several trips he thinks he knows it all, forgetting that these experienced seamen have been at sea for years, and have seen it all. The boils on his arm are turning septic and his temper is becoming increasingly bad. The crew show him no sympathy. They do not take into consideration that this fifteen year old boy is doing the same amount of work as them, experiencing the same conditions and working the same long and arduous hours, on half the pay they get. I feel that if Graham weren't so cheeky, the crew would show him a lot more consideration. I notice that he is very careful about what he says to 'Elvis' and Kelly.

TIME	T°F	WIND	SEA	CONDITIONS ON DECK	REMARKS
1830					Gutting
2030					Hauling
2045					Gutting

As we steam back to our starting point again, we pass the *Ross Leonis*, winner of the Silver Cod Trophy in 1961, 62 and 63.

2300

Up spirits. The deck is clear of fish again and the crew are having tea with their rum. Graham has been to see the Skipper about his boils, but all he can do is to advise him to keep his arm as clean as possible and give him two large plasters. It is difficult enough trying to get a decent wash with the showers and toilets directly aft and the *Oratava* rolling badly and banging her stern down every time she pitches into a heavy sea. Anyway, there's not much time available for washing while fishing. I just try to keep my hands clean, splash water in my face and clean my teeth once a day, when I remember. It's also difficult going to the toilet aft. You have to hang onto the seat with both hands and more often than not, some joker has removed and hidden the top of the toilet cistern, so you suddenly get a cascade of freezing water pouring over you.

TIME	T°F	WIND	SEA	CONDITIONS ON DECK	REMARKS
2315					Shooting away
2330					All square
2400	32°	5	5	Snow squalls, but less water coming inboard	

Day 8 Good Friday 8 April

TIME	T°F	WIND	SEA	CONDITIONS ON DECK	REMARKS
0545	32°	4	4	Very cold	

The wind dropped after midnight, the roll of the ship has lessened considerably and the men have not had to contend with the freezing spray buffeting them all the time.

TIME	T°F	WIND	SEA	CONDITIONS ON DECK	REMARKS
0630				Wind increasing	Hauling

The net is split on the underside. Every time the net is torn, we lose part of the catch, and money.

0650

We are steaming back to our starting point, while the deckhands mend the net. The men are being drenched with spray again because we are at full speed.

0700 – Breakfast

Porridge, fried fish, bread and butter, jam, marmalade. Tea. It has been very cold on deck during the night and the men are ravenously hungry. One young deckhand works his way through porridge, six pieces of fish and two slices of bread and butter and marmalade.

'Course,' says Kelly, 'the most hated men on the ship are the greasers!' Stabbing his breakfast knife in the general direction of one of them, eating his meal and minding his own business. He is rather a small individual who wears an oversize pointed woolly hat on deck. I have seen him in action, and he reminds me of a gnome running about, greasing the winch and other machinery parts, and being careful to avoid Kelly's kicks when he is on the deck. 'Six fuckin' hours on and six off, and all they have to do is run around with their little cans of grease. They really 'ave it off. Don't yer!' And once again Kelly stabs his knife at the unfortunate greaser, who hurriedly finishes his breakfast and leaves the messroom, taking his mug of tea with him.

TIME	T°F	WIND	SEA	CONDITIONS ON DECK	REMARKS
0800					Still mending the net
0830	32°	5	5	Frequent snow squalls	Gutting
0900					Shooting away

In the galley, the Cook and Radio Operator are arguing because the Cook has not made any hot-cross buns. I had forgotten it is Good Friday. It makes me think of home and loved ones. Best not think about them at this stage of the trip though.

0920

I go with the Cook to the cold pantry aft to fetch some stores. The door has a very large padlock on it and when we go in I can see why. It is a large room packed full of food on the shelves and on the deck. There looks to be enough stores to last us three months let alone three weeks. There are large sides of meat, shop size portions of hams and cheeses, hotel size tins of beans, peas and spaghetti and various fruits and hotel size jars of pickled onions, red cabbage, piccalilli and sauces. On the deck there are large sacks of potatoes and other vegetables. There are also large quantities of other foodstuffs, but I don't have time to take it all in.

Back in the galley, I am about to start on the large bucket of potatoes when the Cook asks me to take two mugs of tea to the bridge. This should have been a simple enough task, even for me. I decide to go through the interior of the ship, but halfway across the engine room catwalk, *Oratava* pitches and rolls heavily and some of the tea cascades out of the mugs down into the engine room. Luckily the Chief Engineer is sitting on the starboard side and the hot liquid misses him. He sees me and gives me a somewhat baleful look. The crew are very tolerant with me, but they must think that I am the clumsiest person ever to set foot aboard this ship.

On my second attempt, I decide to go up the ladder to the boat deck and reach the bridge from there. This time I remember the words of a seafaring uncle of mine, 'One hand for yourself, and one hand for the ship, boy?' So, clutching both mugs in one hand and hanging on to the ship with the other, I make my way round to the starboard side. However, I had forgotten that I need two hands to climb this vertical ladder. I can't manage it with one hand.

Finally, I have to take one cup at a time across the engine room gangway and eventually reach the bridge with most of the tea in the mugs.

'Sorry I've been so long. I had a bit of trouble getting it here.' The Skipper and the Radio Operator just exchange glances.

TIME	T°F	WIND	SEA	CONDITIONS ON DECK	REMARKS
1130					Hauling-the net is split again
1145					Mending the net
1200	34°	5		Wind easing. Less water on the deck	All square

Up Spirits – Dinner

Soup, roast beef, roast and boiled potatoes, duff, carrots, peas, cabbage and gravy. Apple pie and custard. Tea.

TIME	T°F	WIND	SEA	CONDITIONS ON DECK	REMARKS
1230					Shooting away
1250					Gutting
1500					Hauling

The cloud is beginning to lift. We can see the mountains for the first time in four days. The sight of the land cheers me up, but the crew say they are sick of the sight of the mountains. The colours look strange though; grey cloud, dark green water, translucent aquamarine just below the wave crests, and the mountains show up orange.

TIME	T°F	WIND	SEA	CONDITIONS ON DECK	REMARKS
1515					Shooting away
1530					Gutting
1745					Hauling – another split in the net
1800	33°	4	4	Snow squalls. The wind is dropping, but so is the temperature	Steaming back. Mending the net

Tea

Another delicious meal – Fried steak and onions, egg, chips and hot cross buns. Tea.

TIME	T°F	WIND	SEA	CONDITIONS ON DECK	REMARKS
1900					Gutting
2045					Shooting away
2100					Two of the deckhands relieve the Skipper in the wheelhouse to allow him an hours sleep
2330					Hauling

Yet another split in the net. This is causing a lot of extra work. But the crew tell me that we have been extremely lucky to have had only one cut out before today. The racing tides and rocky seabed are beginning to tell on the net, which has apparently been in use for the last three trips.

TIME	T°F	WIND	SEA	CONDITIONS ON DECK	REMARKS
2345					Mending the net
2400	29°	3	3	Ice beginning to form on the deck, especially around the fishwasher. Bitterly cold	All square

Today, Graham has been on the deck for a total of sixteen and a half-hours, in temperatures near freezing point and in wet conditions. He is showing signs of irritability and anger. He is smoking more and his face is drawn and paler than usual.

DAY 9 SATURDAY 9 APRIL

TIME	T°F	WIND	SEA	CONDITIONS ON DECK	REMARKS
0230	27°	3	3		

I go on deck to take some photographs of the sequence of hauling the trawl. It is only half past two in the morning, but already there is enough light to be able to switch off the decklights.

TIME	T°F	WIND	SEA	CONDITIONS ON DECK	REMARKS
0545					Decky-learner's watch called out
0600	33°	4 to 5	4	Cold, but the deck is free of water. A bright and pleasant morning	Gutting

In no other job, or on any other type of ship would a fifteen year old have to work the hours in the conditions trawler apprentices do. There is very little colour in Graham's face. There are deep shadows under his eyes and his pupils are dilated. His movements are slow and he looks as if he couldn't care less about his work, and receives a sharp reprimand from the Mate to 'Jump to it!'

0700 – Breakfast

Porridge, fried fish, bread and butter, jam and marmalade. Tea.

TIME	T°F	WIND	SEA	CONDITIONS ON DECK	REMARKS
0800					Gutting
0845					Hauling

There is a bad cut out in the net; in the cod end this time and we lost most of the catch to the voracious gulls, mollymawks and kittiwakes. The Skipper swears violently from the wheelhouse and gives the order to 'bend on' a new and tougher net of nylon.

TIME	T°F	WIND	SEA	CONDITIONS ON DECK	REMARKS
0905				Steaming back to our starting point	All square. The deck crew are cutting the bindings on the old net, and stowing it in the net locker below
0915				Ship steaming at full speed, broadside to the wind. Again the spray is driving across the deck, lashing the men's faces	
1030					Bending the new net onto the 'ground gear' (bobbins, trawl warps, etc)
1205	34°	5	5		Shooting away the new net
1220					Clearing away the tools used for changing over nets

1230 – Up Spirits – Dinner

Dumpling stew, boiled potatoes, onion duff, carrots, peas, gravy, soup, apple crumble and custard. Tea.

Over dinner, the talk is of 'pleasure trippers' or supernumeraries like myself, (who never seem to sail on winter trips!).

'We 'ad this vicar's son come up with us once. When we started fishing', he got 'is rods out and rigged up on t'foc'sle like. We said to 'im, you 'elp us and you can 'ave all the fish ya can carry when we get back. So 'e did. In the end he were swearin' worse than any of us lot. Don't know what 'is old man thought when 'e got 'ome.'

'Yeh, d'ya remember that skipper who had t'take 'is wife along one trip, t'prove he wasn't always going ashore and 'avin other women, and getting pissed all the time? His missus was so sea-sick, they nearly 'ad t'put 'er ashore in Iceland.'

Personally, I can't think why anyone would want to take a 'pleasure-trip' on a trawler.

TIME	T°F	WIND	SEA	CONDITIONS ON DECK	REMARKS
1320					Kelly and Graham on Wheelhouse watch to relieve the Skipper
1400	33°	5	5	Bitterly cold	
1600					Hauling
1615					Shooting away
1630					Gutting
1800	33°	4	4	Still very cold	

Tea

Spaghetti, sausages, fried egg, chips, dumpling stew, soup, bread and butter, jam. Tea.

TIME	T°F	WIND	SEA	CONDITIONS ON DECK	REMARKS
1830					Gutting
1915					

The deck is now clear of fish and the crew sit around in the galley and messroom yarning, drinking tea, smoking and rolling their 'ticklers'. Graham pillows his head on his arms on the messroom table and is asleep very quickly.

TIME	T°F	WIND	SEA	CONDITIONS ON DECK	REMARKS
2000	29°	3	3	Ice forming on the deck	Hauling
2015					Shooting Away
2035					Gutting

I now do something very stupid. I finished off my tin of toffees and chocolates two days ago, and I am desperate for something sweet. I steal a tin of sweetened condensed milk from one of the lockers in the galley. I sit in front of the galley stove spooning it into my mouth as fast as I can, but I get caught. I am halfway through the tin, when the Cook, who I thought had turned in, comes into the galley.

For the first and only time during the trip he is angry. He, quite rightly, reads me the riot act about letting down and stealing from the ship, the Skipper and the crew and that he is very disappointed about what I have done. I can only mutter an apology and offer to pay for it. He points out that there are no shops out here and orders me out of the galley. Luckily for me, he does not tell anyone else about this incident.

TIME	T°F	WIND	SEA	CONDITIONS ON DECK	REMARKS
2300					Hauling
2315					Shooting away
2330					Up spirits

I ask the Skipper if he thinks the rum helps the men to keep going, but he replies that he thinks that the effect is more psychological with hardened drinkers such as these men.

'In a monotonous job like this, all they have to look forward to is the next sleep, the next meal and the next tot of rum.'

TIME	T°F	WIND	SEA	CONDITIONS ON DECK	REMARKS
2335	27°	2	2	Very icy and slippery on deck	Gutting

Day 10 Easter Sunday 10 April

TIME	T°F	WIND	SEA	CONDITIONS ON DECK	REMARKS
0600	32°	2	2	Cold – Ice around the washer – A fine sunny day	Gutting

Everyone has a thick ten-day growth of beard, except for Graham and myself, but this does not hide the fact that their faces are beginning to look drawn, haggard and ashen coloured. There is not a trace of colour on the boy's face and his movements are slow again this morning.

0630 – Breakfast

Porridge, cornflakes, fried fish, bread and butter, jam and marmalade. Tea.

Over breakfast, the Radio Operator tells me that if I want to send a telegram home, to let my family know I'm okay, today would be a good day to do it.

TIME	T°F	WIND	SEA	CONDITIONS ON DECK	REMARKS
0730					Hauling

We brought over 900 stone of fish aboard this haul, the first decent catch we have had according to Kelly. So far we have about 7,000 stone of fish aboard, all prime quality. The Mate tells me that the Skipper is not satisfied; there have been too many small catches and too many net cut outs and splits, which have wasted fishing time.

TIME	T°F	WIND	SEA	CONDITIONS ON DECK	REMARKS
0745				Steaming Back	Gutting
0910					Shooting away
0925					Gutting
0947				EMERGENCY STOP!	

I have just thrown some vegetable peelings over the side when the ship starts to vibrate and shudder violently. We shudder to a stop, the screw still trying to push the ship forward. Emergency bells are ringing throughout the ship, the engine room telegraph clangs several times and I can hear the Mate shouting to the deck crew to lay flat. I do the same. We have started to heel over to starboard. When we begin to go slowly astern the *Oratava* begins to recover from her list.

Our net has caught and held fast on an obstruction on the seabed. Luckily for us, we stopped before the trawl warps parted. The Skipper swings the *Oratava* in a wide circle to starboard at slow ahead, then we stop and begin to haul the trawl, very slowly at first. Whatever the obstruction was, it has ripped part of the underside of the net, but we still have about 80 stones of fish in the cod-end which is still intact.

The shock of the sudden stop has jolted us all out of our usual stupor, induced by the monotony of our work. The decky-learner is now working faster than he has been for the past two days.

TIME	T°F	WIND	SEA	CONDITIONS ON DECK	REMARKS
1010					Mending the split net
1035					Shooting away
1050					Gutting

Just before lunch, I take the message I want to send home up to the

The boat deck

radio room. The Radio Operator looks at the paragraph I have composed in disbelief.

'Bloody 'ell, kid! It costs three and seven[1] a word ya know, and that includes yer address.' We swiftly cut the message down to four words.

As I leave the wheelhouse by the portside door and begin to make my way aft via the boat deck, I notice thick brown smoke billowing out from under the boat deck. I run back to the bridge.

'Er, Captain, I think we're on fire!'

'What!? Where?'

Steaming into a snow squall

'Near the boat deck aft.'

'Oh aye that'll be the cod liver oil boiler. It's always sparkin' off. Tell one o' the deckies to see to it, will ya?'

I go down on deck and report the fire to Kelly.

'Oh, aye, it's always catching fire. We'll see to it.'

I'm surprised that everyone is taking this fire so casually judging by the amount of smoke pouring away to port. I go and look for myself. The cod liver oil boiler is a large circular metal drum situated as far aft as you can get, under the boat deck. It is heated underneath and boiling oil is seeping down the sides of the container from under the lid and catching fire. This is producing the large amounts of thick brown obnoxious smelling smoke. Eventually one of the deckhands comes along and adjusts the temperature controls. Well, I could have done that for them.

The cod liver oil boiler catches fire quite regularly during the rest of the time we spend on the fishing grounds.

TIME	T°F	WIND	SEA	CONDITIONS ON DECK	REMARKS
1155					Up Spirits
1200	33°	2	2	Cold	

Dinner

Roast chicken and stuffing, onion duff, roast and boiled potatoes, peas, carrots, cabbage, gravy, soup. Chocolate duff and custard. Tea.

Over dinner, I'm idly looking at the cutaway diagram hanging over one of the bulkheads, showing the *Oratava*'s interior layout and giving her specifications. At the top of the diagram is her name when she was first launched – *St Christopher*, and I suddenly remember that it is the name of the patron saint of all travellers. Well, it's a good omen, but it does not make me feel any safer. I'm still expecting some major disaster to befall us. It's a good job you can't see into the future, because in twenty-one months' time, one of her sister ships, *St Romanus*, will be lost with all hands in atrocious winter weather conditions north of Iceland.

TIME	T°F	WIND	SEA	CONDITIONS ON DECK	REMARKS
1300					Gutting
1330					Hauling
1350				Steaming back	Gutting

After washing up I am free for about an hour and a half, and now that the weather has calmed down I go up on the boat deck for half an hour each afternoon. Already the deck, lifeboat and self-inflating liferafts are covered in bird droppings.

The days are fine and sunny now, but there is no warmth from the sun and it is very cold. The sea is a dark blue colour and I find the sight of land, the mountains of Norway away to the east, very comforting. The water is very clear and leaning over the guardrail you can see a long way down. There appear to be very large jellyfish swimming about, which I thought lived only in warmer waters. This is also a good vantage point to see the trawl being hauled in. On the foredeck, or up in the wheelhouse, I always seem to be getting in someone's way.

Even with a vest, a tee shirt, two thick sweaters and a duffel jacket, the cold soon starts to penetrate and after half an hour and two cigarettes, I go below again.

TIME	T°F	WIND	SEA	CONDITIONS ON DECK	REMARKS
1515					Shooting away
1530					Skipper relieved on wheelhouse watch
1745	28°	1	1	Icing up on the deck and washer	

Early Tea

Chicken soup, ham, pork, corned beef, chips, fried tomatoes, fruit and custard, bread and butter, jam. Tea.

TIME	T°F	WIND	SEA	CONDITIONS ON DECK	REMARKS
1845					Hauling
1900					Standing by to shoot away

Usually the trawl is put back over the side as soon as the net has been emptied of fish, but not this time. We are steaming around in circles, and the Mate explains to me that the Skipper is now after the largest shoals of fish. The deckhands, with nothing to do but wait and smoke, are stamping their feet and complaining of the cold, and it is cold, very cold.

TIME	T°F	WIND	SEA	CONDITIONS ON DECK	REMARKS
1930	27°	1	1	There is no wind, but it is bitterly cold	Shooting away
1950					Gutting
2110					Hauling

A short tow this time. The Skipper is changing his tactics as we are not catching much fish. After we have hauled and the Mate has performed his usual task of pulling the slip-knot beneath the cod end of the net, and moving swiftly out of the way as the fish cascade onto the deck, he discovers that some of the bobbins, which hold the mouth of the net open on the seabed, have been damaged when we came fast this morning.

They will have to be replaced at once. This is going to cost us more fishing time. As darkness falls and the deck floodlights are switched on, Graham and I spend the next hour filling the net needles with twine as fast as we can (and that's not fast enough for the Mate and one or two other deckhands), and running round the ship collecting the various tools required from the engine room and foc's'le.

TIME	T°F	WIND	SEA	CONDITIONS ON DECK	REMARKS
2125					Replacing the bobbins
2230					Shooting away
2245	26°	1	1	Ice forming on the mast and rigging	Up spirits

Even I manage to down half a tot of rum tonight without choking and gagging all over the place. The hour's work in the cold rarefied air has done me a lot of good, and I now feel fitter that I have done since the start of the voyage. I had a bad cold when I came aboard, which disappeared two days after we crossed the Arctic Circle, and Kelly has reassured me several times that being violently seasick 'Does yer a power o' good, cos it gets rid of them old poisons and bile in yer stomach. You'll go home fit as a fiddle.'

Several of the crew take advantage of the five minute 'up spirits' break to go below to put on more layers of clothing to combat the ever-increasing cold. For the umpteenth time I wonder how anyone can stand this job in winter.

TIME	T°F	WIND	SEA	CONDITIONS ON DECK	REMARKS
2250					Gutting
2400	25°	1	1		Watch below

The deck is now clear of fish and the crew thankfully strip off their oilskins and kick off their seaboots and go below for an hour's sleep and warmth. Once again, I am thankful that I can go below and sleep for a few hours, at a time when the body's metabolism is at its lowest – midnight to four o'clock – 'the graveyard watch' sailors call it.

There will be at least two hauls, maybe three before breakfast, and in an hour's time, some of the crew will have to turn out and go back on deck again, where it is still getting colder.

Notes

1. Three shillings and seven pence (old money).

Day 11 Easter Monday 11 April

0545

The 6 a.m. to midnight watch have just been called out. One of the decky-learner's boils broke during the night and the Skipper puts a bandage and waterproof dressing on it. The other boil is large and inflamed with two septic heads.

The monotony and grind are beginning to tell on the men. They are all 'fed up to the teeth' this morning. The decky-learner is complaining of aching muscles and joints. His eyes are bloodshot and now and again he puts his hand to his head as though he is dizzy.

TIME	T°F	WIND	SEA	CONDITIONS ON DECK	REMARKS
0600	33°	1	1	A good bright cold calm morning	Gutting

0700 – Breakfast

Porridge, fish, bread and butter, jam, marmalade. Tea.

No one is talking over breakfast this morning, they are all too tired for conversation. Now I drop my second big clanger of the trip. Momentarily forgetting the ship's runner's advice, I voice my thoughts aloud, 'Mm, morale looks a bit low this morning.'

As soon as the words are out of my mouth, I realise my mistake. What a thing to say to tired men! Elvis looks at me in exasperation. 'Write that in yer fuckin' little book and it'll go over the side and you'll be followin' it!'

One or two of the crew nod in agreement.

'Oops, sorry.'

I make a swift exit from the crew's messroom. I am really going to have to watch it. That's two bad mistakes I've got away with. I had better not make a third one.

TIME	T°F	WIND	SEA	CONDITIONS ON DECK	REMARKS
0800					Hauling
0815					Shooting away
0830					Gutting
1030					Hauling
1045					Shooting away
1105					Gutting

I'm called up on deck and I make my way there with some trepidation. Surely they are not really going to throw my notes and me over the side? I need not have worried. They must have forgotten what I said at breakfast this morning, because they want to show me the six-foot long basking shark, which was caught in the net during the last haul. Although they have the shark hanging from the wheelhouse gantry, they are quite gentle with it and have lashed a couple of ropes around its body so as not to harm it.

'Just run yer 'and along its back,' says Kelly.

I find the skin very rough and very abrasive.

'If yer did that real quick yer'd flay all the skin off the palm of yer 'and. Now, this is what they like.'

Kelly picks up a broom and gently proceeds to scrub the shark's back. It wriggles. I hadn't realised it was still alive!

Then the shark is swung over the side and lowered carefully into the sea. The slipknots on the ropes are loosened and the shark swims away, none the worse for his visit to the *Oratava*. On the way back to the galley, I realise, yet again, that I could have run and got my camera to photograph the shark, if only I had remembered.

TIME	T°F	WIND	SEA	CONDITIONS ON DECK	REMARKS
1145					Up Spirits
1200	35°	1	1	Good	

1200 – Dinner

Roast beef, roast and boiled potatoes, carrots, peas, swedes, onion duff, gravy, soup. Fruit and custard. Tea.

TIME	T°F	WIND	SEA	CONDITIONS ON DECK	REMARKS
1300					Gutting
1330					Hauling
1345					Shooting away
1405					Gutting
1530					Deck clear of fish. Skipper relieved on wheelhouse watch
1630					Hauling – net torn
1645					Mending the split net
1705					Shooting away
1720					Gutting
1800	34°	1	1	Good	

Up on the boat deck this afternoon I started to think of all the things I could have been doing at home on this Easter Monday afternoon. Then I stopped because it doesn't do to think about home out here, you just need to get on with things. On the good side, this is the eleventh day of the voyage, so maybe we are halfway through the trip. I am very glad the Skipper asked me to help out in the galley, it helps to pass the time. If I didn't have this work time really would be dragging. But we do seem to have been out here a long time, we have just had our third weekend at sea. The crew are used to it, but I'm not. They have not had a weekend ashore for months.

They tell me that for the past three or four trips, the *Oratava* has docked at 5 a.m. on a Wednesday and sailed again on the early morning tide two days later on the Friday, giving them slightly less than forty-eight hours ashore between each three week voyage. The only way they could get more time off would be to sign off the ship. They are reluctant to do this as James Nunn always comes home with a decent catch which sells for a good price.

Thinking back reminds them of what happened to the previous deck-learner four trips ago. During a hauling operation, the boy tripped over one of the 'pound' boards.[1] Putting his arm out to break his fall, he unfortunately landed with one of his hands on a moving trawl warp. He lost the top of his thumb and his hand was so badly flayed that they had to take him into the nearest Norwegian port with a hospital.

'The kid just sat there, staring at 'is thumb 'till the mate whipped 'is sou'wester[2] off and put it over 'is 'and. We stopped the winch and the skipper came down with the first aid bag, and gave 'im a jab of morphine.'

It was only later that I found out from the Cook that the crew had a 'whip round' and gave the boy all the money they had, and that the Skipper had gone to the hospital with him and made arrangements to get him home before sailing out to the fishing grounds again.

Tea

Liver, egg, chips, cold ham and pork, cheese, bread and butter, jam. Tea.

TIME	T°F	WIND	SEA	CONDITIONS ON DECK	REMARKS
1900					Gutting
1930					Hauling

The 'doors' have twisted and jammed against the ship's side and once again it is the experienced Kelly and the Mate who lean over the side with long crowbars and a sledgehammer, hammering away at the door by the forward gallows to try and dislodge it. When they succeed in freeing the door it slams back against the ship's side and they only just have time to roll out of the way.

TIME	T°F	WIND	SEA	CONDITIONS ON DECK	REMARKS
1955					Shooting away
2010					Gutting
2100					Watch below

There were not many fish in the last haul, and now the deck is clear, the crew are having a mug of tea in the messroom. The decky-learner quickly gulps down his tea, lights yet another cigarette, (during the past week, his smoking has increased from half an ounce to an ounce of tobacco each day) and heads for his bunk for an hour.

TIME	T°F	WIND	SEA	CONDITIONS ON DECK	REMARKS
2230					Hauling
2245				Steaming – East	Up Spirits
2315					Shooting away
2330					Gutting
2400	33°	2	2	Cold and calm	

Notes

1. One foot high sections of wood arranged across the deck, into which the catch is emptied.
2. Fisherman's oil skin hat.

Day 12 Tuesday 12 April

TIME	T°F	WIND	SEA	CONDITIONS ON DECK	REMARKS
0600	31°	4	4	The wind from the north is freezing	Gutting

We have been fishing for a week now and the strain is really beginning to tell on the young decky-learner and one of the older deckhands who goes by the name of 'Old Tom'. They were called out at 0550 hours and for their first quarter of an hour on deck their movements are very slow – they are both moving like old men, shuffling about with bowed heads and shoulders. It is the freezing, bitterly cold north wind, which penetrates their fatigue, and soon they are working fairly fast in order to keep warm. All the deckhands are complaining of the cold. I have got a warm scarf tied around the lower part of my face, but I can feel the cold making my teeth ache.

The thermometer I am taking the temperature readings from is lashed to the top of the ladder leading to the boat deck, on the starboard side of the ship, aft. But I am beginning to realise that the temperatures on the main foredeck where the crew work are probably lower than the ones I am recording, especially when the ship is steaming into the wind. Temperatures on the main deck could be five or six degrees lower. The best place for my thermometer would be on the mast, but as I would probably get in the way, it will have to stay where it is.

0700 – Breakfast

Porridge, fish, bread and butter jam, marmalade. Tea.

Nothing tastes right this morning. I put my dish of porridge to one side and can only manage half a slice of bread and butter and jam, but I am very thirsty. Kelly has been watching me push the food aside, and the amount of tea I am drinking.

'It's all the salt in the air, y'know. Mind, by the time we get 'ome, you'll be as fit as a fiddle. All this fresh sea air, and you've got all them old poisons and bile up outa yer stomach when you was bein' sick.'

I mention how tired Graham and 'Old Tom', (who are on the 0730 second sitting, for breakfast) looked when they first came on deck this morning.

'Aye, well the kid's got ter get used to it, but 'Old Tom' ... 'e's about forty-five or forty-eight now. 'E's bin at it thirty odd years now, thirty years on the deck, and nothin' much ter show for it.'

I thought 'Old Tom' was about sixty. The hardship and strain of this life are beginning to tell on this man.

TIME	T°F	WIND	SEA	CONDITIONS ON DECK	REMARKS
0800					Hauling
0815					Shooting away
0830					Gutting
1030					Hauling
1050					Shooting away
1105					Gutting
1155					Up Spirits
1200	34°	2	2	Still very cold	

Dinner

Dumpling stew, boiled potatoes, savoury duff, carrots, peas, cabbage, gravy, soup. Rice pudding and jam. Tea.

Each crew member has half an hour for each meal. Just enough time to eat, drink a mug of tea, and smoke a rolled up cigarette. Then it's time to haul on your sea boots, oilskins and gutting gloves and get back out into the cold for another five or six hours.

TIME	T°F	WIND	SEA	CONDITIONS ON DECK	REMARKS
1300					Gutting
1330				Another split in the net	Hauling
1345				Steaming – east	Mending the torn wing in the net
1430					Shooting away
1545					Hauling
1600					Shooting away
1615					Gutting
1645					Hauling

An even shorter trawl – only half an hour, instead of the average two and a half to three hour trawl. The men can't understand the Skipper's tactics.

'What the fuck's he up to?'

This from more than one deckhand. The men are swearing even more bitterly than usual because of the increased number of hauls. Despite the aid of the winch and the forward and aft gantries, it is heavy work manhandling the nets and the crew are very tired now.

TIME	T°F	WIND	SEA	CONDITIONS ON DECK	REMARKS
1630				Steaming south-east	Gutting

We have crossed and recrossed these fishing grounds, searching for larger shoals, and as the Skipper says, what shows up below the ship on the echometer is not necessarily caught in our net, which is half a mile astern of us. Every time the net comes up damaged, there are some heartfelt curses from the Skipper in his customary position every time the trawl is hauled or shot, leaning out of one of the starboard side wheelhouse windows. From this position he can see anything that goes wrong and can, if necessary, stop the winch from the wheelhouse. He can also spot and quickly warn the men of any dangerous waves heading towards them, especially during the critical times of hauling and shooting the trawl.

Now we are steaming hard to the south-east, still looking for larger shoals of fish and better catches.

TIME	T°F	WIND	SEA	CONDITIONS ON DECK	REMARKS
1800	33°	1	1	Cold and calm	

Tea

Fried bacon, sausages, tomatoes, chips, dumpling stew (left over from dinner) cheese, bread rolls (baked during the afternoon) fruit and custard, bread and butter, jam. Tea.

TIME	T°F	WIND	SEA	CONDITIONS ON DECK	REMARKS
1815				Still steaming south east	The deck is now clear of fish – because of only moderate hauls
1900					Shooting away
1915					All square – watch below

Everyone, including me, heads for their bunk after the trawl has been shot away. Usually, the deckhands share a pot of tea and have a smoke, before going below to snatch an hour's sleep. But not tonight, everyone is too tired.

TIME	T°F	WIND	SEA	CONDITIONS ON DECK	REMARKS
2200					Hauling
2215					Shooting away

Day 13 Wednesday 13 April

TIME	T°F	WIND	SEA	CONDITIONS ON DECK	REMARKS
0215	27°	2	2	Cold and calm	

I succumbed to sheer tiredness last night and fell asleep at 7.30 p.m. The sound of the trawl doors crashing against the ship's side finally woke me up. It's uncanny to step on deck at 2 o'clock in the morning in almost broad daylight.

TIME	T°F	WIND	SEA	CONDITIONS ON DECK	REMARKS
0545					0600 to midnight watch called out
0600	30°	1	1	Good	Gutting

Graham stumbles out onto the deck, drugged from sleep and from the lack of it. His movements are slow and fumbled. He keeps dropping his gutting knife, and misses the washer several times when he tries to throw the fish into it. His face is ashen, as are the faces of the rest of the crew.

0700 – Breakfast

Porridge, fish, bread and butter, jam, marmalade. Tea.

Few of the crew eat breakfast today. They say they are too tired to eat and spend their half-hour meal break drinking tea and smoking.

TIME	T°F	WIND	SEA	CONDITIONS ON DECK	REMARKS
0800				Intermittent snow showers	Hauling
0815				Steaming	Gutting
0930					Shooting away
0950					Gutting
1105					Skipper relieved on wheelhouse watch
1145					Hauling

Having snatched half an hour's precious sleep, the Skipper is back in the wheelhouse to supervise the haul, and this time it is a good catch – about 900 stones of fish. We now have about 12,500 stones of fish aboard – just enough to meet the expenses of this Arctic voyage.

'Good, now we can start fishin' for ourselves,' says Kelly.

TIME	T°F	WIND	SEA	CONDITIONS ON DECK	REMARKS
1215	33°	1	1	Good	Up Spirits

Dinner

Soup, roast beef, roast and boiled potatoes, cabbage, peas, swedes and gravy. Jam duff and custard. Tea.

The crew are no longer eating the huge amounts of food they consumed when we arrived on the fishing grounds. They eat a smaller portion at each meal. Even eating is becoming an effort for some of them now. I look across the table at 'Old Tom'. He is only forty-seven, but with his grey beard and haggard, ashen face, he looks at least sixty years old.

TIME	T°F	WIND	SEA	CONDITIONS ON DECK	REMARKS
1245				Steaming	
1330					Shooting away
1350					Gutting

During the afternoon a Dutch 'long-liner' fishing vessel passes us heading south. It is an easier method of fishing with lines and hooks, but you do not catch as much fish as you do on a trawler. I have seen very few British trawlers up here while we have been on these fishing grounds. Now and again we sight the *Ross Renown* which sailed on the same tide as us from Grimsby two weeks ago. It seems a lot longer than two weeks. I try to keep busy to make the time pass more quickly, but I am starting to get bored with the monotony, even though you never know what is going to happen next. Even the sign of the Norwegian mountains is beginning to pall. I would feel better if I knew when we were going home, but we don't, and we won't until the Skipper makes the decision. At the rate we are catching fish, it may be some time before we make a good profit on the trip.

TIME	T°F	WIND	SEA	CONDITIONS ON DECK	REMARKS
1600					Hauling
1615					Shooting away
1630					Gutting
1800	33°	1	1		Good

Tea

Spaghetti, eggs, bacon, chips, savoury pancakes, cheese, bread and butter. Tea.

Another delicious meal. One thing I am going to miss when I get home is all this excellent food. Over tea, we learn that one of the greasers has had an argument with the Chief Engineer during the afternoon. He is now on strike, fast asleep in his bunk. Kelly rises to the occasion.

'So,' he says, stabbing his knife in the direction of the owner of the large, pointy woollen hat, 'Yer mates gone on strike, 'as he? Well, you'll have ter work double watches for a start. Typical 'in it. You two 'ave got the easiest fuckin' job on the whole fuckin' ship 'an 'e has ter go on fuckin' strike. Well, 'e'll be on bread and water 'till he decides to start workin' again, if he starts workin' again. Mind you, this is mutiny really, 'im refusin' to work, like. Well 'e'll 'ave ter go on trial won't 'e. Yeh, we'll 'ave ter 'ave a trial.'

Kelly carries on triumphantly in this vein throughout the meal, feeling that his opinion of greasers has now been thoroughly vindicated. But no one is really listening to him, and we never do find out why the greaser went on strike, or what the argument with the Chief Engineer was about. What is becoming clear is that the monotony and fatigue are leading to irritability and frayed tempers, and I make another mental note to be increasingly careful about what I say or do.

TIME	T°F	WIND	SEA	CONDITIONS ON DECK	REMARKS
1905					Hauling
1920					Shooting away
1935					Gutting
2120					Deck clear of fish

With the gutting finished from the last haul, the deck crew quickly make their way below to snatch half an hour's rest and sleep, without pausing for the usual mug of tea and a cigarette.

TIME	T°F	WIND	SEA	CONDITIONS ON DECK	REMARKS
2200					Hauling
2215				Steaming	Gutting
2320					Shooting away
2335,					Up spirits
2340					Gutting
2400	32°	1	1	Cold and calm	

Day 14 Thursday 14 April

TIME	T°F	WIND	SEA	CONDITIONS ON DECK	REMARKS
0700	36°	1	1	Good – Sunshine and snow showers	

This is the fourteenth day out from Grimsby and the ninth day on the fishing grounds and hauls have been extremely poor during the night. The Skipper is looking very worried. Some skippers would have taken it out on the crew, finding extra jobs for them on the deck, but James Nunn lets his men sleep. The deck is clear of fish and most of the crew are below.

0715 – Breakfast

Porridge, fish, bread and butter, marmalade and jam. Tea.

TIME	T°F	WIND	SEA	CONDITIONS ON DECK	REMARKS
0740					

Graham's watch has just been called out for breakfast, but only the engineers are eating this morning. I am finding the breakfast meal of porridge and fried fish a bit monotonous now. The extra sleep has cheered up the crew. The decky-learner's movements are less slow this morning and once again he is foolishly cheeking some of the crew.

TIME	T°F	WIND	SEA	CONDITIONS ON DECK	REMARKS
0815					Hauling
0830					Shooting away
0850					Gutting
1100					Hauling
1115					Shooting away
1130					Gutting
1200	38°	1	1	Good	Up Spirits

Dinner

Meat pie, onion duff, boiled potatoes, cabbage, peas, swedes and soup. Apple crumble and custard. Tea.

TIME	T°F	WIND	SEA	CONDITIONS ON DECK	REMARKS
1400					Hauling
1415					Shooting away
1430					Gutting

Another poor catch and today's previous catches have not been very good. It has only taken the crew an hour to gut and stow each haul and then spend the rest of their time between hauls sharing wheelhouse watches. This, on a day when working conditions are good on deck. It is a fine sunny day, and although the temperature is still low, less than 40°F, it feels warmer, and the sea is almost a flat calm.

It takes only three-quarters of an hour to gut the last haul. The deck is again clear of fish and the crew are in the messroom drinking tea and yarning. They tell me that with the hauls we are now catching, we are likely to be another two weeks out here. Leaving me with that cheering thought they go below for another hour's sleep. They have this ability to snatch half an hour or an hour's sleep whenever the opportunity arises. I don't and the next hour really drags until it is time to go and help the Cook with the tea. I spend the time smoking three cigarettes and leafing through a pile of *Dandy* and *Beano* comics (property of the engine room).

TIME	T°F	WIND	SEA	CONDITIONS ON DECK	REMARKS
1700					Hauling
1715					Shooting away
1735					Gutting
1800	37°	2	2	Good	

Tea

Bacon, eggs, liver, tomatoes, chips, cheese, bread and butter, jam and marmalade. Tea.

TIME	T°F	WIND	SEA	CONDITIONS ON DECK	REMARKS
1830					Second watch to tea
1900					Gutting
1940					Wheelhouse watch
2030					Hauling
2045				Steaming west	Gutting
2130					Shooting away
2150					Gutting
2300					Hauling
2315				Steaming south west	Gutting
2400	34°	2	2	Heavy snow showers	Up Spirits – Watch below

Not a successful fishing day. The trawl has been hauled eight times during the past twenty-four hours, with poor results for all the hard work. Even though the deck crew have worked shorter hours today, the decky-learner has still worked for a total of thirteen-and-a-half hours during his eighteen-hour watch.

Day 15 Friday 15 April

TIME	T°F	WIND	SEA	CONDITIONS ON DECK	REMARKS
0100					Dawn breaking
1000	37°	3	3	Good – another fine sunny day	

Most of the crew have been asleep since midnight, only being called out for wheelhouse watches. We are still steaming south-west. The Cook thinks the Skipper is going to try his luck off Scomvaer in the Lofoten Islands.

TIME	T°F	WIND	SEA	CONDITIONS ON DECK	REMARKS
1200	38°	3	3	Good	Up Spirits

Dinner

Soup, roast beef, roast and boiled potatoes, peas, cabbage, Yorkshire pudding and gravy. Chocolate duff and custard.

Despite their long sleep, the crew are ill-tempered, with splitting headaches. They tell me that the cause of their headaches is the extra or 'gash' sleep as they call it. Two of the deckhands nearly came to blows during dinner. They both had double helpings of rum because they missed their tots last night, and this plus their bad tempers because of their headaches, led to a trivial argument over how to tie a certain knot. But the argument escalated into an ugly scene. Other crew members stopped it by reminding them that they needed to settle their argument forward on the deck, not here in the messroom. Tempers and nerves are extremely frayed today.

The greaser who went on strike two days ago, is now at work again after seeing the Skipper. He comes in to the second sitting for dinner looking rather sheepish. No one questions him or makes any remarks, so we will never know what the argument with the Chief Engineer was about, or what the Skipper said to him.

TIME	T°F	WIND	SEA	CONDITIONS ON DECK	REMARKS
1315					Shooting away
1335					Wheelhouse watch
1600					Hauling

Not a big catch – only about 50 stones in the net. The Skipper swears violently to himself. I hope we have not wasted fourteen hours and 150 miles of diesel fuel for more bad catches.

As the net was coming aboard, the decky-learner, who should know better by now, got in the way of the Third-hand who was working the winch. The Third-hand had to push Graham aside quickly and roughly to prevent an accident. The boy swore at the Third-hand, who would have struck him if the Skipper had not shouted down from the wheelhouse: 'Leave 'im!'

TIME	T°F	WIND	SEA	CONDITIONS ON DECK	REMARKS
1615					Shooting away
1630					Gutting
1800	37°	1	1		Good

Tea

Ham, spam, corned beef, chips, eggs, cheese, soup, jelly and custard, rolls and butter, jam and marmalade. Tea. (Once again our Cook surpasses himself!)

There was more trouble for the decky-learner at the start of the second sitting for tea. Now he has refused to work because he says he is being badly treated by his shipmates. He was nearly involved in a fight with Kelly, who was trying to get a mug of tea from the galley hatchway. Without meaning to, Graham got in his way, twice. In a fit of temper, Kelly grabbed the boy by the shoulders and half pushed and half threw him across the messroom. At once, the rest of the crew grabbed hold of Kelly and Graham to prevent any further trouble. Graham has refused to have his tea in the same room as Kelly and has gone below to his bunk. If only the boy would look where he is going.

After he has eaten his tea, the Mate goes to report the incident to the Skipper, who tells him to leave the boy in his bunk until tomorrow.

TIME	T°F	WIND	SEA	CONDITIONS ON DECK	REMARKS
1915	33°	3	3		Hauling

I go on deck with a bucket of slops to throw over the side, just in time to see a massive haul of fish. The cod end of the net always surfaces first because of the air trapped inside the bodies of the fish, but this time the cod end shoots high into the air like a whale breaching before plunging back into the sea. The trawl net is absolutely full of large cod and is lying on the surface. There is a big grin on the skipper's face and the crew are looking very pleased as well. This catch is worth a lot of money.

The crew lean out to lash the mouth of the net together. There are so many fish, the cod end will have to be swung aboard several times before the trawl is emptied.

TIME	T°F	WIND	SEA	CONDITIONS ON DECK	REMARKS
1955					Shooting away
2010					Gutting

As I am helping the Cook to clear away after tea, I have an idea. They will be one man short on deck until midnight, because Graham has refused to work, so why don't I go and help out? The Cook looks a bit doubtful when I ask him, but when I have finished in the galley, I borrow an old oilskin and put on the brand new seaboots which I have not worn all the trip and go on deck.

I ask Kelly if I can help. He too, looks a bit doubtful but fetches me some old gutting gloves and a razor sharp gutting knife. He shows me what to do, expertly cutting down the belly of a fish, throwing the entrails over the side, tossing the liver into a basket and then throwing the fish up into the washer. He makes it look easy, but when I go to pick up a large cod, I get a surprise. I get hold of the fish by the tail and it flips back and nearly hits me on the nose as I bend to pick it up. I know the fish still had some life in them, but I did not realise how much. Now I know. I look for a smaller fish and try to gut it cleanly and quickly but I am not very successful. When I try to throw it into the washer I miss that completely. My efforts at trying to gut several more fish are far worse than my early attempts to get unspilt mugs of tea to the wheelhouse – I can just about manage that satisfactorily now.

Young Tom finally comes across to me and suggests that they might be needing some help down in the fish hold. I take off my oilskin and go down. The Mate and a deckhand are expertly packing fish neatly into steel trays with a bed of ice in them and then scattering ice on top before storing them on shelves. When I ask them if they would like some help they suggest I chop some ice for them. The ice-making plant situated on the forward bulkhead is continuously producing the ice. Well, I should be able to manage this simple job okay.

I take a swing at the large block of ice with the very large axe, which practically bounces back off the ice. Right! There is obviously a technique to this. I am just about to take another swing when the *Oratava* lurches up on a wave and I just avoid knocking the Mate on the head with the axe.

'Watch yerself, young man!'

'Oops, sorry.'

I spend the next half hour chopping ice, being very careful to keep the axe well away from the Mate and the deckhand but it is difficult to judge the movement of the ship down here and I lose my balance several times. After I have spent half an hour chopping and falling over, the Mate suggests that I go up to the galley to make a brew of tea for the watch.

My foray onto the deck has not been very successful. The crew make it all look easy, but it's not and I guess it's too late into the voyage for me to acquire the skills necessary for the deck. Anyway, I haven't got the stomach for gutting fish, which are still alive.

TIME	T°F	WIND	SEA	CONDITIONS ON DECK	REMARKS
2200					Hauling

Another massive haul of fish. Again the net is absolutely full and again the cod end shoots up into the air before crashing back into the sea. By the time all of the catch has been swung aboard, the fish pounds are full and overflowing. Several of the crew tell me I must be a lucky bastard!

TIME	T°F	WIND	SEA	CONDITIONS ON DECK	REMARKS
2240					Shooting away
2255					Gutting

We now have about 18,000 stone of fish aboard, a fair catch to take home.

TIME	T°F	WIND	SEA	CONDITIONS ON DECK	REMARKS
2350	33°	2	2		Up spirits – on deck

Day 16 Saturday 16 April

TIME	T°F	WIND	SEA	CONDITIONS ON DECK	REMARKS
0600	36°	1	1	Good	Gutting

Another bright sunny morning, and a calm sea, but no one is in the mood to appreciate these fine weather conditions.

The Skipper has had a talk with Graham this morning and he is now back at work looking rather sheepish and embarrassed. The twelve-hour sleep of last night and the night before have refreshed him, but there is not a trace of colour in his face.

As I was coming on deck this morning the Cook warned me to treat the crew very carefully. Catches have been excellent during the night but the men have not left the deck since midnight and they are tired and irritable. The Cook also warns Graham, who has already realised what kind of mood the men are in. He keeps very quiet and is careful not to get in anyone's way.

0700 – Breakfast

Porridge, fish, bread and butter, jam and marmalade. Tea.

The crew are complaining because of the heavy catches: 'We want hard work at the start of the trip, not now it's nearly over!'

At the second sitting for breakfast, the worst incident of the voyage occurs. The greaser who went on strike comes into the crew's messroom and switches on the radio, tuned to the BBC World Service. A couple of minutes later Kelly comes in and promptly switches the radio off again: 'Hey, I were listenin' to that.'

The greaser, a tall well-built individual, stands up and switches the radio on again.

In the ensuing argument between Kelly and the greaser, insults are exchanged and the argument becomes so heated that Kelly draws his gutting knife. The greaser picks a knife up from the table to defend himself. For a moment it looks like blood is going to be spilt. Once again it is the protests from the rest of the crew and the unwritten rule about settling grievances and arguments forward on the deck, that put a stop to the argument.

The greaser throws the knife back on the table, picks up his mug of tea and storms out. The rest of the breakfast break is very quiet.

TIME	T°F	WIND	SEA	CONDITIONS ON DECK	REMARKS
0810					An extra tot of rum for the crew
0815					Hauling
0830					Shooting away
0850					Gutting
1035					Hauling
1050				Steaming – west	

The Mate has just reported to the Skipper that some ice will have to come up out of the fish room before any more fish can be stowed away below. The Skipper tells the Mate to get every available hand, including myself, to help shift the ice.

TIME	T°F	WIND	SEA	CONDITIONS ON DECK	REMARKS
1100	39°				Shovelling ice

It is a very warm day – for the Arctic, and soon we are all stripped to our shirtsleeves and sweating profusely. We have formed a chain-gang of shovellers to bring the ice up from the depths of the fish room, across the fish room to the hatchway, up and through the hatchway onto the deck and then over the side, one bucket at a time! After a quarter of an hour of this, my back and arm muscles are aching from the unaccustomed use of the shovel, and we are all gasping for breath. It's a good job it is nearly dinnertime.

TIME	T°F	WIND	SEA	CONDITIONS ON DECK	REMARKS
1145					Up Spirits
1200	40°	2	2	Warm	One watch to dinner

Dinner

Soup, dumpling stew, savoury duff, boiled potatoes, swedes, peas, cabbage, carrots. Jam duff and custard. Tea.

TIME	T°F	WIND	SEA	CONDITIONS ON DECK	REMARKS
1230					Shovelling ice

Back in the fishroom I wish I hadn't eaten the dumplings, the savoury duff and the jam duff, which are all sitting pretty heavily in my stomach. You hardly get enough time to eat your meal aboard a trawler, let alone begin to digest it.

TIME	T°F	WIND	SEA	CONDITIONS ON DECK	REMARKS
1300					Shooting away
1320					Shovelling ice
1430					Gutting

It has taken ten of us two hours to get the necessary amount of ice up out of the hold. As we emerge from the fishroom aching and sweating and very glad to get finished 'Old Tom' says, 'You have to take everything in your stride.'

This piece of homespun philosophy does not go down well with the rest of the crew who tell him in no uncertain terms what they think about the job we have just finished.

TIME	T°F	WIND	SEA	CONDITIONS ON DECK	REMARKS
1600					Hauling

The Skipper invites me up to watch this haul from the vantage point of the bridge. Considering how tired he is, it is very considerate of him to allow me to go up there. In my rush to get to the bridge before the winch is started, I forget my camera. Every time there is something worth photographing I forget the damn camera, and I am never going to come this way again. When I get there, the Skipper points to the starboard corner of the wheelhouse.

'Stand over there, me old son.'

Making sure that I am well clear of the ship's wheel and engine-room telegraph, in case he needs to get to them quickly. He leans out of one of the starboard windows and gives the order to start the winch.

Despite the open window, it feels very warm up here. The Skipper has stripped down to his string vest, 'Fear naught' serge working trousers and his slippers. His massive chest and arms are a clear indication of years of hard labour on the deck before he got his Skipper's ticket. He has a wet towel wrapped round his head and explains that the cold drops of water running down his face help to keep him awake. He has also stuck a cigarette paper on each of the bridge windows because: 'I've smashed that many pairs of glasses tryin' to get me 'ead through a window that's been closed, and me thinking it was open.'

He tears off a strip of paper, about four inches wide and eighteen inches long, hanging out of the echometer, the ship's fish finding asdic, and hands it to me.

'Souvenir for ya.'

He points out the seabed and the fish shoals which are clearly indicated on the roll of paper.

'Mind, you must remember that this shows what's underneath the ship and yer net's half a mile to three quarters astern. What yer steam over, may not get caught in the trawl.'

He spends the next ten minutes making various helm adjustments, making sure that *Oratava*'s starboard side remains the leeward side so that the trawl will stay clear of the ship until it is winched aboard. At the same time he keeps a watchful eye on the deck, the wires, the winch, the men and the sea to port and starboard. At the moment there is very little wind and only a slight swell. It must be a hell of a job, keeping the ship steady in bad weather during this critical manoeuvre. He lights another of the sixty cigarettes he smokes each day.

We have another good catch although the net is torn on the underside. We also have part of another trawl net wrapped around our cod end, with half a dozen of the heavy iron rollers still attached to it. We will have to keep this wreckage until we sail into deeper water. The Skipper sends me down to help Graham fill the net needles and as I am leaving the bridge he tells me that once we have begun our homeward voyage I can come to the bridge at any time and make full use of the ship's log for my study.

TIME	T°F	WIND	SEA	CONDITIONS ON DECK	REMARKS
1620				Steaming – west	Mending the net
1705					Shooting away
1720					Gutting
1800	41°	1	1	Good	

Tea

Fried liver and onions, eggs, chips, tomatoes, cheese, biscuits, soup, bread and butter, jam and marmalade. Tea.

We are just finishing our meal when the Mate puts his head around the door. There is a big grin on his face as he tells us that we are steaming home after the next haul. I have never felt more relieved before (or since!). This is definitely the best moment of the trip for me, but I try to emulate the crew who never show any emotion at all if they can help it. They are trying to keep nonchalantly straight faces, but they can't help grinning at each other.

TIME	T°F	WIND	SEA	CONDITIONS ON DECK	REMARKS
2000	39°	1	1	Good	Hauling

The last haul, and it's another good catch. As soon as the net is emptied onto the deck for the last time the otter-boards are hoisted inboard and secured and we turn for home. As we turn south we pass four Russian trawlers in line ahead steaming north, silhouetted against the sunset. I dive below for my camera, but by the time I get back on deck they are too far away for a decent photo.

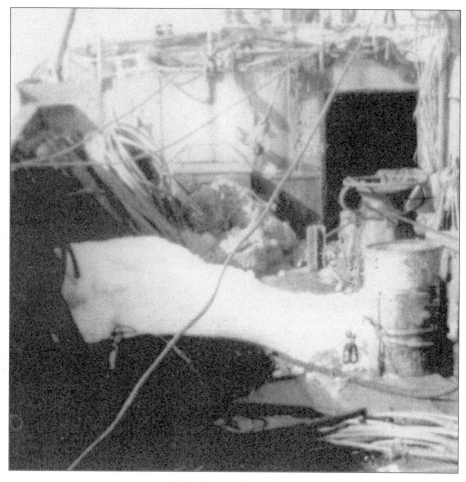

The last of the ice

TIME	T°F	WIND	SEA	CONDITIONS ON DECK	REMARKS
2030					Gutting
2300					Stowing and lashing the net

Soon after the last fish have been stowed away below, the horde of noisy seabirds, our constant companions for the last two weeks, turn away from the ship. A few stay with us for a few more miles until they too wheel away to the north. The Skipper switches the radio through to the deck loudspeaker system after the crew's request for some music.

TIME	T°F	WIND	SEA	CONDITIONS ON DECK	REMARKS
2400	36°	1	1		

DAY 17 SUNDAY 17 APRIL
HOMEWARD BOUND FROM FUGLEHUK TO GRIMSBY

TIME (GMT)	GYRO COMPASS	OVERHEAD COMPASS	DISTANCE (MILES)	WIND FORCE	SEA (STATE)	POSITION
0015						Up Spirits

In the wheelhouse, the Skipper has another wet towel tied turban fashion around his head, the drops of water running down his face helping to keep him awake. During the twelve days we have been on the fishing grounds, he has averaged less than four hours sleep every day. He is responsible for the safety of the ship and the crew and he has to be on the bridge for every haul of fish. He chain smokes and the meals that the Cook brings up for him are often left untouched.

TIME (GMT)	GYRO COMPASS	OVERHEAD COMPASS	DISTANCE (MILES)	WIND FORCE	SEA (STATE)	POSITION
0025						

After a ten-minute break for their rum, a mug of tea and a cigarette, the crew continue to dismantle the fish washer and fishpounds and to hose down and tidy up the deck.

TIME (GMT)	GYRO COMPASS	OVERHEAD COMPASS	DISTANCE (MILES)	WIND FORCE	SEA (STATE)	POSITION
0110						Abeam Skomvaer – 59 miles

Now that we have left the coast of Norway and are in deeper water off the fishing grounds, the crew are throwing the remnants of the wrecked net we trawled up yesterday, over the side. Young Tom is picking up the heavy iron rollers one by one and dumping them overboard. Even the Skipper is impressed with his strength:

'There y'are, the next contender for Cassius Clay!' Now that is an interesting thought.

TIME (GMT)	GYRO COMPASS	OVERHEAD COMPASS	DISTANCE (MILES)	WIND FORCE	SEA (STATE)	POSITION
0300	208°	SW × W	76	1	1	

The crew have just gone below to sleep. Some of them have been on deck since midnight on Friday and are desperately tired. The hours and work would have been bad enough without that backbreaking slog of getting the ice up out of the hold.

The Bosun, Graham and I are sharing the wheelhouse watch. I am feeling too euphoric to sleep now that we are on our way home.

TIME (GMT)	GYRO COMPASS	OVERHEAD COMPASS	DISTANCE (MILES)	WIND FORCE	SEA (STATE)	POSITION
0415						

I am supposed to be keeping a lookout to starboard, but I am not paying too much attention to the empty sea. I should be, because suddenly the bows of a very large freighter loom into my vision. Luckily for me, they are obviously keeping a better bridge watch on the freighter. The large vessel, flying the Norwegian flag, her decks gleaming with ice, overtakes and passes us half a mile away. The Bosun says she's probably come down loaded with coal from the mines in Spitzbergen.

TIME (GMT)	GYRO COMPASS	OVERHEAD COMPASS	DISTANCE (MILES)	WIND FORCE	SEA (STATE)	POSITION
0700	208°	SW × W	123.5	2	2	T°37°F Snow Squalls

Breakfast

Porridge, fish, bread and butter, jam, marmalade. Tea.

The deckhands are all fast asleep, the only crew members eating breakfast are the engineers and radio operator.

TIME (GMT)	GYRO COMPASS	OVERHEAD COMPASS	DISTANCE (MILES)	WIND FORCE	SEA (STATE)	POSITION
0730						

The Mate and a very tired looking deckhand come up to relieve us on wheelhouse watch. Graham and the Bosun go below and I go to help the Cook. I have to throw a lot of wasted food over the side.

'It's sod's law,' says the Cook. 'If I 'adn't cooked enough for all the crew, they'd all be getting' up wantin' their breakfast.'

TIME (GMT)	GYRO COMPASS	OVERHEAD COMPASS	DISTANCE (MILES)	WIND FORCE	SEA (STATE)	POSITION
1200	210°	SW¾S	182	2	2	T°40°F Up Spirits

Dinner

Chicken, roast and boiled potatoes, peas, cabbage, swedes, gravy, soup. Chocolate duff and custard.

A few very tired looking deckhands turn out for their tot of rum and eat small portions of food. Apart from those on wheelhouse watch, they go straight back to their bunks. I throw a lot more food over the side. Again the Cook impresses on me that other skippers would find jobs for their crews, instead of giving them a well-deserved rest.

TIME (GMT)	GYRO COMPASS	OVERHEAD COMPASS	DISTANCE (MILES)	WIND FORCE	SEA (STATE)	POSITION
1800	210°	SW¾S	253.5	2	2	

Tea

Soup, ham, spam, chips, fruit and custard, biscuits, bread and butter. Tea.

All the crew turn out to eat, but there is none of the usual meal time yarning and banter. The Mate comes in to tell us that the Skipper is giving away the rest of the ship's bond after tea. It is the usual pecking order and by the time Graham and I get to the bridge there are only bars of soap and tins of soup left – the beer, cigarettes and tobacco have already gone.

On the way below the Bosun grabs us. 'Right lads, there's heavy weather ahead. We've got to batten down and make everything secure.'

Well, we can see another whiteout ahead, but we have been running through snow squalls all day and the sea is fairly calm. We follow the Bosun onto the foredeck busily looking for things that need securing. But everything has been secured already and all the hatchways have been closed, secured, covered with tarpaulin and battened down. While we are looking for things to do, thick snowflakes begin to swirl around us, but it only takes about a minute to sail through the snow squall – the Bosun's 'heavy weather'.

'Right lads,' says the Bosun glancing up at the bridge, 'that'll do then.'

As Graham and I make our way aft, I realise that the Bosun has been doing his best to impress the Skipper with his keenness and efficiency, ever since the episode with the fishwasher while we were steaming north. Unfortunately for the Bosun, the Skipper was not at all impressed with us running round the deck in a snow storm and remarked to the deckhand on watch with him: 'What the 'ell's 'e up to now?'

TIME (GMT)	GYRO COMPASS	OVERHEAD COMPASS	DISTANCE (MILES)	WIND FORCE	SEA (STATE)	POSITION
1900						

Apart from the sound of the engines, it is very quiet around the ship. Those not on wheelhouse or engine room watch are all resting below. Even the Cook has decided to have an early night. The snow squalls increase in frequency and duration, and some time before midnight we cross the Arctic Circle again.

TIME (GMT)	GYRO COMPASS	OVERHEAD COMPASS	DISTANCE (MILES)	WIND FORCE	SEA (STATE)	POSITION
2300	210°	SW¾S	325.5	2	2	
2400						T°36°F Snowing hard – Up Spirits

Day 18 Monday 18 April

TIME (GMT)	GYRO COMPASS	OVERHEAD COMPASS	DISTANCE (MILES)	WIND FORCE	SEA (STATE)	POSITION
0300	210°	SW¾S	358	1	1	
0400	210°	SW¾S	370	variable 1	1	
0500	A/C 190°	SW¾W	382	2	2	
0700	190°	SW¾W	408	2	2	
0730						T°38°F

Breakfast

Porridge, fish, bread and butter, jam and marmalade. Tea.

As usual, after prolonged sleep, after hours of heavy prolonged work, the deckhands are not in the best of moods, not talking much and complaining of headaches. This morning, they are all on deck with the Mate and the Bosun, splicing wires, quite a skilled job.

TIME (GMT)	GYRO COMPASS	OVERHEAD COMPASS	DISTANCE (MILES)	WIND FORCE	SEA (STATE)	POSITION
1100						T°40°F

It is a very warm day, and uncomfortably hot in the cabins. In the galley the temperature is up to 90°F and the Cook and I are dripping with sweat. We never seem to get a happy medium, we are either too cold or too hot.

The whole ship is shaking and reverberating as we steam at full ahead, with the engineers trying to squeeze an extra knot from the pounding engines.

TIME (GMT)	GYRO COMPASS	OVERHEAD COMPASS	DISTANCE (MILES)	WIND FORCE	SEA (STATE)	POSITION
1200	190°	SW¾W	462	2	2	T°42°F – Up Spirits

Dinner

Roast pork, roast and boiled potatoes, peas and carrots, onion duff, soup and gravy. Rice pudding and jam.

TIME (GMT)	GYRO COMPASS	OVERHEAD COMPASS	DISTANCE (MILES)	WIND FORCE	SEA (STATE)	POSITION
1300						

This afternoon work begins with giving the *Oratava*, a thorough clean, inside and out. After I have finished clearing away and washing up I go down to help Kelly scrub out the alleyway by our bunks. He opens a cupboard door next to our bunks, which I never realised was there, although I have passed it time after time during the voyage. It is just like our broom cupboard at home, filled with an assortment of brooms, mops, scrubbing brushes and cleaning fluids. He hands me a mop, a broom, a bottle of disinfectant and a bucket with a length of rope lashed to the handle.

'Right, go and fetch a bucket of seawater. Don't lose the bucket or you'll 'ave ter pay for a new one. I'll be getting' these gratings up.'

I throw the bucket over the side and get a shock, because I nearly follow it overboard. The speed of the ship and the rapidly filled bucket create a powerful drag. I have been at sea for nearly three weeks, but I am still making bad, and in this case, near fatal, mistakes.

By the time I get back to Kelly with the bucket only three-quarters full, he has lifted the heavy gratings out onto the deck and is hosing them down. He pours a liberal amount of disinfectant into the bucket and tells me to give the alleyway a good scrubbing with the broom and them mop it dry. He goes to join the rest of the deckhands who are washing down and scrubbing the decks and salt-caked upperworks of the ship. The hardest to get clean is the boat deck, which is almost completely covered in bird droppings.

TIME (GMT)	GYRO COMPASS	OVERHEAD COMPASS	DISTANCE (MILES)	WIND FORCE	SEA (STATE)	POSITION
1600				3	3	T°42°F Snow squalls

My next job this afternoon is to join Graham in the wheelhouse cleaning the inside of the windows and then the brasswork. There is quite a lot of brass to polish; the compass, the binnacle, the engine room telegraph and other bits and pieces. I ask the Skipper if he thinks we will be going through any more gales. He looks at me in amazement. 'Why, do ya want a gale?'

He tells me that he has got a film at home he took aboard the *Oratava* in severe gale 9 to storm Force 10 conditions. I would have liked to have seen that.

I find all this cleaning up tedious and a bit of an anti-climax, and I am glad to get back to the galley.

TIME (GMT)	GYRO COMPASS	OVERHEAD COMPASS	DISTANCE (MILES)	WIND FORCE	SEA (STATE)	POSITION
1830						T°40°F

Dumpling stew, fried egg, corned beef, chips, cheese, biscuits, bread and butter, and jam. Tea.

The deckhands are all looking much better now and are far more cheerful than they were at breakfast. Old Tom and another deckhand sit planning a visit to York races when we get back.

'I bet you two don't get any further than the third pub in Rigby Square,' says Kelly derisively.

Graham is recovering from the strain of the work on the fishing grounds. His eyes are clearer and there is some colour in his cheeks. His boils are beginning to heal up.

The Mate tells me we should be docking in Grimsby early on Wednesday morning, so I go up and send another brief telegram home, telling my family when I should be arriving home. I never realised you had to pay for the name and address on the telegram as well as the message!

Anyway, only one more day to go!

TIME (GMT)	GYRO COMPASS	OVERHEAD COMPASS	DISTANCE (MILES)	WIND FORCE	SEA (STATE)	POSITION
2300	190°	SW¾W	589	4	4	
2330						Up Spirits
2400						T°38°F Snow squalls

DAY 19 TUESDAY 19 APRIL

TIME (GMT)	GYRO COMPASS	OVERHEAD COMPASS	DISTANCE (MILES)	WIND FORCE	SEA (STATE)	POSITION
0300	190°	SW¾W	635	East 6	6	
0700		SW¾W	681	East 8	8	

We are still at full steam ahead and the easterly gale is causing the *Oratava* to roll violently. We are back in the North Sea with its shallower bottom causing the shorter swells and some very large waves. I was looking forward to this last full day at sea, but it is not going to be a good one. I must have talked this gale up.

I am ordered to stay out of the galley, not because I have done anything wrong, it's too dangerous for me to be in there. There are heartfelt curses coming from the galley as the Cook and Graham, who has been assigned to help him today, try to keep the food from spilling. There are clamps and battens to hold the pots and pans on the stove, but boiling water hisses out from under the lids. The galley has become the most dangerous place on the ship.

TIME (GMT)	GYRO COMPASS	OVERHEAD COMPASS	DISTANCE (MILES)	WIND FORCE	SEA (STATE)	POSITION
0730						

Breakfast

Cornflakes, fish, bread and butter, marmalade. Tea.

TIME (GMT)	GYRO COMPASS	OVERHEAD COMPASS	DISTANCE (MILES)	WIND FORCE	SEA (STATE)	POSITION
0830						

The crew go to work cleaning out the alleyways and cabins and disinfecting them. I'm not working this morning. I am finding the motion of the ship very difficult. I have not had any breakfast as I am feeling decidedly queasy again. They say that one way to prevent seasickness is to look at a fixed line, like the horizon, but today when you can see the horizon, it is a mass of ragged waves.

I sit in the crew's messroom for a while and then go out and stand in my usual position for being sick by the starboard gallows. We are passing close by a trawler hove to and riding out the gale. I watch as the trawler disappears completely behind a large wave as we go down into a trough. The *Oratava* heels over to starboard and buries her rails under the water. The sea sweeps inboard soaking me up to my waist. It is a good job that I have got one arm wrapped around the gallows as I can feel the seawater pulling at me as it recedes back through the scuppers and over the side. A strong hand grabs the back of my sweater and pulls me back. It's Kelly.

'Well, I did tell yer ter keep to the lee side. Ya best get changed then come up ter the wheelhouse.'

Even up in the wheelhouse the motion of the ship makes things difficult for me and I wedge myself against the portside windows. The wind and sea is still rising and I hang on as the ship goes over to port so far, it seems as if the wheelhouse windows are going to touch the water. Seeing the alarm on my face one of the crew says: 'Don't worry, she'll come back,' and she does, heeling back far over to starboard. I'm starting to get the other sort of seasickness now. It's like a very bad headache, as if tight bands of iron are being clamped across my forehead. I eventually finish up back in my bunk, in the same state as I started the voyage, flat on my back watching my jacket hanging on a hook at the end of my bunk swinging from left to right as the *Oratava* rolls from starboard to port. What a way to finish the voyage.

TIME (GMT)	GYRO COMPASS	OVERHEAD COMPASS	DISTANCE (MILES)	WIND FORCE	SEA (STATE)	POSITION
1200	183°	SW¼W	737	East 9	9	Up Spirits

Dinner

Roast beef, boiled potatoes, cabbage, peas, carrots, and gravy. Apple crumble and custard.

Despite the severe Gale Force 9, the Cook and Graham have managed to produce dinner and the crew manage to eat it. The bad weather continues throughout the afternoon and I spend most of my time in my bunk, while the crew finish cleaning the interior of the ship.

TIME (GMT)	GYRO COMPASS	OVERHEAD COMPASS	DISTANCE (MILES)	WIND FORCE	SEA (STATE)	POSITION
1800	183°	SW¼W	806	East 8	8	

Tea

Ham, corned beef, eggs, chips, biscuits, bread and butter. Tea.

The crew have finished their work and spend the evening in the messroom smoking and drinking. Only now can we allow our thoughts to turn to home and loved ones, conversations between shipmates about them, too private to write in this log.

TIME (GMT)	GYRO COMPASS	OVERHEAD COMPASS	DISTANCE (MILES)	WIND FORCE	SEA (STATE)	POSITION
2300	175°	S × W	870	East 7	7	Up spirits

DAY 20 WEDNESDAY 20 APRIL

TIME (GMT)	GYRO COMPASS	OVERHEAD COMPASS	DISTANCE (MILES)	WIND FORCE	SEA (STATE)	POSITION
0100	170°		891	6	6	Abeam Flamborough Head

At last! The day I have been waiting for. As we close the land the wind and sea lessen, but there is still enough motion to keep us sliding about in the shower room. We are all washing and shaving off the accumulation of three weeks' dirt and beards. It's difficult keeping yourself clean aboard a trawler because you never seem to get time for a proper wash.

TIME (GMT)	GYRO COMPASS	OVERHEAD COMPASS	DISTANCE (MILES)	WIND FORCE	SEA (STATE)	POSITION
0300	170°		910	4	4	
0400	Variable		923.7	3	3	Abeam Spurn Lightship – Dawn breaking

Ship's Log Closed Down

Epilogue

IT IS HALF PAST FOUR and a grey dawn, overcast, with low cloud cover, just like when we sailed out three weeks ago. We are all ready to go ashore, and many of the crew are wearing expensive well-cut suits. It feels good to wear a shirt again after weeks of itchy vests and sweaters.

Young Tom tells me the Skipper wants to see me on the bridge. I climb up the after-companionway and make my way along the boat deck for the last time. In the wheelhouse the Skipper asks me, 'Well, d'ya think you could make a career out of this game then?'

I smile and shake my head, 'No Skipper. I don't think I would be able to stick it in winter, and it's the three weeks out and only two days ashore which would get me.'

'H'mm. Okay. Thanks for what you've done back there this trip. I'll pay for your bond and your telegrams home.'

'Thank you very much.'

But Kelly said he would pay me £20 as well, and I have done a lot of work. That's a disappointment.

We are racing up the Humber, the Chief and Second Engineers still striving to get more speed out of the *Oratava*. We overtake every vessel except the Rotterdam-Immingham Car Ferry which overhauls us. Graham and the four deckhands on the foc'sle, 'preparing' the mooring lines (a job which actually only needs two men) give the Ferry and its passengers some very rude gestures and lewd comments.

I'm looking upriver towards Grimsby, where I can just make out the famous clocktower landmark, when the Skipper says, 'Just look at those silly bastards.'

We are so close to home now, but the crew have finally come to blows. A fight has broken out on the foc'sle. Graham wisely comes down and makes his way aft. As he passes the bridge, the Skipper leans out of the wheelhouse window, 'What's up?'

Apparently, there were three cans of beer left, and there are four of them.

By five o'clock we are approaching the lock gates. The Skipper takes the wheel, rings down for half-speed and swings the *Oratava* in a wide turn to port. He rings for slow ahead and spins the wheel back to midships. Losing way (slowing down) all the time we pass through the lock gates and into the inner harbour and docks. We are approaching the fish dock and make another slower turn to port. The Skipper puts the engine-room telegraph over to 'Stop' and lets the incoming tide push the *Oratava* gently up to the quayside. The mooring lines are thrown ashore and we are made fast to the quay by the bows. He rings down for 'Finished with Engines'. It is a quarter past five.

'Well, that's it, me old son. Hope you enjoyed the trip then.'

I thank him once more for letting me come on the voyage and go below to get my two bags. Kelly had mentioned a crew photograph, but some of them are scrambling ashore already. Kelly is waiting for me below.

'Well, I think you stood up to the trip pretty well.'

I never expected this kind of praise from him and I am really pleased.

'Thanks!'

'Now, what about your sea-boots? You've hardly worn 'em. I can get two pound ten shilling for 'em down the dock. No more'n that mind.'

I imagine he may get more than that, but that's okay by me. Kelly beats a hasty retreat with the boots.

'See ya down the office then, nine o'clock.'

I come up on deck and to my amazement, a customs officer is there.

'Anythin' to declare then?'

My mouth drops open in surprise and he backs off.

'Okay, okay I 'ave ter ask y'know.'

I say goodbye to my shipmates and the Cook tells me that Graham and the greaser are both getting the sack for refusing to work during the trip.

As it is now high water, in order to get off the *Oratava* I have to climb up to the foc'sle, go over the safety rail and climb down a battered old wooden ladder lashed to the rail, rather an undignified exit after where we've been.

To my surprise, Graham is waiting for me and invites me home for breakfast. I accept, but as we walk towards the line of waiting taxis, my legs nearly give way and I start to roll about like a drunk. Graham steadies me and grins, 'Well, ya nearly got yer sea legs, now ya gotta get yer land legs back again.'

I'm not the only one rolling about. Several taxis are disgorging trawlermen in various states of intoxication, about to sail. One man is staggering about so badly he has to be helped.

'Cor,' says Graham, ''E's the Chief Engineer of the *Northern Isles*. 'Ope the Second's (Second Engineer) okay.'

At the taxi, Graham turns to look back at the *Oratava*. He will never get another job on that ship, or with the Abunda Fishing Company again. The Skipper will give him a bad discharge on his papers, and he may have difficulty finding a berth with a decent fishing company again. He does not realise this yet, although the skipper has already fired him verbally this morning.

'Oh, look at that, a bastard Icelander! Why do they let them land here, when they've got a twelve mile limit and we can't always get a good price on what we land. Stupid bastards!'

A large Rejkavik trawler is berthing alongside the *Oratava*. It's a good job Kelly and Elvis are already ashore or the knives would be out!

Graham lives in a little back street near the docks and we arrive at his house at 7.30. His mother and brothers and sisters sit quietly around us as we tuck into eggs, bacon and fried bread. Graham tells his mother that he is going to sign off the *Oratava* and join another trawler company.

'Iceland, next trip, Mum, and the midnight sun.'

His mother just nods and smiles a quiet knowing smile. We get another taxi, (trawlermen never waste time walking anywhere if they can help it, during their precious forty-eight hours ashore), for the short journey to the offices of the Abunda Fishing Company. We arrive there just after nine o'clock. Other crew members are already there busy counting their hard-earned money.

In the four hours since we docked, the catch, including the raw cod-liver oil, has been landed and sold on the Grimsby Fish Market. We brought in 2,200 kits, or 22,000 stones of fish, which sold for £10,500 – a successful voyage not only in terms of the fish we caught, but the price they were sold for as well.

Graham gets £49 10s. before tax, the deckhands £99 before tax and the Skipper gets a lot more. He will be paid 10 per cent of the catch after expenses and he also has a quarter share in the *Oratava*. He should have earned over £2,000 before tax. The rewards are certainly there, if you can be successful in this business.

The crew thought this trip was an 'easy one' (we had good weather most of the time) compared with average trips and a 'holiday' compared to what they go through in winter.

For once they are sympathetic towards me because I didn't get paid any wages and there are many offers to 'come and have a drink'. Soon they will be queuing up waiting for opening time at ten o'clock.

Kelly has been waiting for me and hands me the two pounds ten shillings for the sea-boots. 'Coming for a pint, then?'

Reluctantly I have to refuse. It will take me four to five hours to drive back home in my very unreliable second-hand car. (These are the days of unscrupulous car dealers, and I bought my car from one.) Also I have heard tales of men being plied with a lot of drink and then being shanghaied. I don't want to end up in the scuppers of the *Oratava* when she sails on the Friday morning tide again.

I go round to the car park behind the offices and suddenly realise why everyone and everything looks different. I have been clear of pollution for the past three weeks, especially north of the Arctic Circle, and now I am back in the industrial haze[1] of the Midlands, even here on the east coast.

On my way out of Grimsby, I call in to see Christine Holroyd. She's back at college already, but her mother says she's very glad to see that I am back safely and that they have been worrying about me (so have I!). I thank her again for her kindness and for Mr Holroyd's help, and say that I hope to see her again.

I get back into my rusty green and white Ford Poplar and head for the A16 and home.

Deep in the Lincolnshire Wolds, I am admiring the red earth of the freshly ploughed fields and thinking how good it is to see green grass and trees again, when I am pulled over by a police patrol car. (Good job I didn't go for a drink with the crew!) I get out of the car.

'What's up?'

'We've stopped you under the 1962 Road Traffic Act. Those sills on your car don't look very safe. Is your hand brake on?'

The two policemen put their weight against the back of my car and push. Luckily, the handbrake holds.

'Where are you going, sir?'

'Great Yarmouth.'

'Where have you come from?'

'Grimsby, I've just come back from a fishing trip to the Arctic,' I tell then proudly.

'Oh, some kind of fisherman are you? We thought you were some kind of student.'

I never went back to Grimsby. I always said I would, but I never did. I did read the *Trawling Times* regularly. James Nunn became President of the Grimsby Trawlers Federation later on in 1966. The *Oratava* was sold to a South African Fishing Company in 1968. She continued fishing until she was scrapped in 1983.

Three more distant water trawlers capsized, sunk by ice top hamper in January 1968, one of them within the shelter of Isafjord, Iceland. Only one man, the mate of the *Ross Cleveland*, survived. Questions were at last asked in Parliament concerning the safety and stability of British Trawlers.

In January 1974, the stern trawler *Gaul* disappeared off the North Norwegian coast, close to the border with Russia.

The investigation into that sinking is still ongoing.

For my special study, 'Endurance Under Arctic Conditions', the college gave me a B+ with the comments: 'A most interesting log'. Another student spent two nights copying out of two books from the college library for his thesis: 'Greek Athletics'. He got an A+ with the comment: 'An excellent thesis'.

They got really uptight when I refused to publish my study, and told them why. 'Think of your career, and how this study could enhance the prestige and reputation of the college, etc, etc.'

Maybe.

But I had given my word and I kept it, and I'm glad I did.

Notes

1. Stopping at Sheffield station in November 1964, I had to close the train window because of the fumes from the factory chimneys belching out black, grey, white, yellow, brown and even reddish coloured smoke.

Endurance and Fatigue

I OFTEN WONDERED during my voyage on the *Oratava* how on earth the deckhands could stick the life they led, the monotony of three or more weeks at sea, and only forty-eight hours ashore between these long trips. And so I asked them and was given various reasons.

'Well, we're lucky. We don't have to worry about getting to work on time everyday. It's already 'ere.'

'I tried workin' in a factory once. Couldn't stick it. Better off out 'ere. Too many small minded gits ashore.'[1]

''Cos, it's a good free life out 'ere. Long as yer knows yer job and get on with it, no fucker bothers ya!'

'I did try workin' ashore, couldn't stick it.'

'Well, there's fuck all to look forward to workin' ashore, is there?'

'Because there's nothing better than comin' in out of a gale of wind and ridin' steady up the 'umber, knowin' ya got a load o' money comin' and two days to spend it in. Ya wouldn't get that ashore, would ya?'

''Cos, I'm gonna be a Skipper.' (The decky-learner.)

'I tried workin' on a farm once. When it came ter' pay day, I knew how much I 'ad ter give the missus. There were just enough left over for a packet o' fags or a pint. I needed the fags, but I were dyin' o' thirst. I said t'farmer, "will yer give us a sub outa next week's money, like?" The mean bastard said No. I shipped out next day.'

'We can earn twice, maybe three times the money we'd get ashore.'

'But what about what you go through in wintertime up north?' I asked.

The crew were more reticent in talking about voyages in the winter, but Kelly volunteered.

'It's a fuckin' bastard in winter. There's no daylight in December and January up the White Sea. Yer workin' under decklights all the time yer fishin'. Fuckin' bastard job it is then.'

That was all they were prepared to say.

Then one of the crew answered an unspoken question I hesitated to ask, when he said quietly.

'We're okay, but it's not fair on our families really, we spend so much time at sea. My kids hardly know me. It's like a stranger walkin' into the 'ouse every three weeks for them.'

'I know,' said another deckhand. 'I've got three kids. I don't know 'ow I got 'em. I'm usually too pissed or too tired to know what I'm doing half the time I'm ashore.'

What surprised me was the fact that the crew actually felt sorry for more lowly paid workers ashore, although some expressed contempt as well. Then they thought of some more reasons why they were trawlermen.

''Cos people pay hundreds of pounds to come up 'ere ter see this scenery. We get paid ter see it!'

'I don't know any other way of life.'

'There was no where else to go.'

'Because we're two day millionaires!'

The fact remains that life aboard a trawler, especially in winter, was so intolerable that only a small percentage of humanity was able to endure it. In the 1960s, out of the total male working population, there were only eight thousand trawlermen, most of them born to the life. There were those who tried the job, but lacked the qualities necessary to stand the life. Very few men who lived outside the fishing communities of Fleetwood, Grimsby and Hull succeeded as distant water trawlermen.

In 1962, a Hull sociologist estimated that one third of the trawlermen were the sons and grandsons of fishermen. Most of the others came from fishing families and the vast majority lived in the fishing communities.[2]

You needed both the physical strength to endure the long hours on deck and the necessary mental attitude to survive each long hard voyage and then go back for more. On the *Oratava* I observed men with the necessary physical strength to withstand the eighteen hour days. I also saw the build up of fatigue. There were no accidents, but reactions were slow at times, notably when the *Oratava*'s net caught on an obstruction on the seabed.

Following the losses of three distant-water trawlers in the Arctic in January 1968, one of the recommendations made by the 1969 Holland-Martin Committee of Inquiry concerned the hours of work and rest periods on distant, middle and near water vessels. In addition they recommended that there should be research into the effects of fatigue on crews, and any links between excessive fatigue and the high accident and loss rate.

The Holland-Martin Report calculated that the standard mortality for trawlermen was seventeen times that of the male population as a whole, while those trawlermen aged from fifteen to forty-five were twenty times more likely to die as a result of an accident at work.

The Medical Research Council's studies undertaken by Dr Ruffel Smith of conditions aboard a distant water stern freezer in March/April 1971[3] and aboard a distant water side fishing trawler in February 1972,[4] did not reveal any links between fatigue and accidents.[5]

The Report of the Working Group on the Occupational Safety of Fishermen published in 1979, noted that the available accident statistics did not indicate that accidents were more frequent during the later stages of a voyage when the deckhands might be expected to be more fatigued. Therefore, in the absence of positive evidence, the majority of the Working Group decided it was not appropriate to 'take these matters further within the Group.'[6]

But the Transport and General Workers Union representatives on the group, and, at a later stage, the Merchant Navy and Airline Officers Association on behalf of the Grimsby Trawler Officers Guild took a different line. While agreeing that the problem of the fatigue level/accident rate had been inadequately researched, they drew attention to the statement of the Holland-Martin Committee that 'the opinion of medical experts with whom we had discussed the question, supports the common-sense view that excessive fatigue considerably increases the probability of accidents, especially in hazardous occupations' – and reinforced this by references to the experiences of their members.

But by 1979, it was all getting a little too late. I am sure that Dr Smith on his two winter voyages observed crew fatigue. I certainly did. I saw, on the eighth day of the voyage, a boy at the start of his watch, so dazed with tiredness that he had to be spoken to two or three times before he realised anyone was talking to him.

I also observed at the end of the sixteenth day, that the deck crew were showing signs of extreme exhaustion. In my Summary of the Voyage, I have detailed the fatigue factor and the causes I observed, concentrating mainly on the fifteen-year-old decky-learner.

Notes

1. In December 1962, I saw a young fisherman, who had decided to work ashore for the winter, throw down his broom in disgust and march out of a Norfolk sugar beet factory. He had been given three different jobs by three different individuals within the space of twenty minutes.

2. c. f *The Rise and Fall of Deep Water Trawling*, Austin Mitchell and Anne Tate.

3. But the hours worked aboard this type of vessel were less than on the side-fishing trawlers.

4. But this was only one voyage.

5. No, because there were no accidents on these two particular voyages.

6. *Report of the Working Group on the Occupational Safety of Fishermen*, Department of Trade (HMSO, London 1979).

A Summary of the Voyage Compiled from the Ship's Log and my own Log

Outward Bound

0400 hours
Friday, 1 April 1966

2045 hours
Monday, 4 April 1966

DURING THE VOYAGE from Grimsby to North Norway, Graham Quantrill, the fifteen-year-old deckhand apprentice, worked for an average of eight hours a day on deck. The weather improved from moderate to good, and temperatures on deck during the day gradually dropped from 50°F to 40°F as the ship proceeded to latitude 71°N. This gave Graham and the crew time to adapt themselves to fine weather conditions during the Arctic day, but not to the more severe night temperatures and bad weather conditions.

At times Graham was engaged in extremely heavy manual work, manhandling nets up from the hold and lifting heavy metal objects, but because of his height of five feet eleven inches, and extremely good physique, he showed no signs of strain or tiredness, apart from heavy breathing and a slight perspiration, which normally accompanies heavy work. By the time we arrived on the fishing grounds, he looked perfectly fit and well with clear eyes and a good colour of the face.

On the Fishing Grounds

2045 hours
Monday, 4 April 1966

2015 hours
Saturday, 16 April 1966

In the first three days on the fishing grounds, the crew were working in almost gale force conditions. The Force 7 winds, which lowered the average temperature to 30°F, brought continuous sleet and snow squalls, which drove almost horizontally across the deck.

The decks were continually awash, and conditions were especially bad during hauling operations. The weight of the net pulled the ship over, and the crew had to work thigh deep in water against the rail at times.

Graham averaged six hours sleep out of twenty-four, and worked for an average of sixteen-and-a-half hours a day. At the end of this period he was suffering from two large septic boils on his arm and was in a thoroughly bad temper. He was inclined to cheek his shipmates and was not at all popular with them. They had no sympathy for him, and seemed to ignore his age and the fact that he had to work as hard as everyone else.

During the next three days, the high wind and seas lessened, but the cold increased, and at night temperatures dropped to 26°F, causing the additional hazard of slippery ice forming on the deck.

Graham began to show signs of strain on the fourth day on the fishing grounds, and other crew members on the fifth and sixth days. The signs of fatigue I noticed were: a pallor of the face, slower, less well co-ordinated movements, irritability, chain smoking, and an increase in repetitious use of bad language.

The worst periods of fatigue for Graham were immediately after his inadequate periods of rest. He was usually called before breakfast, but would be unable to eat this meal, even after a short working period on deck in the fresh air. He would just sit with his head bowed over a mug of tea and smoking a cigarette. During the early part of the time spent fishing Graham appeared to overcome his fatigue after about an hour on deck, and he would be able to move faster with better co-ordinated movements. But this period of extreme fatigue gradually increased to about three hours.

On the seventh day, the men were complaining bitterly about their work and wishing that they were home. Graham was suffering from aching muscles and joints. At breakfast his eyes were bloodshot, and I noticed symptoms of dizziness in his actions.

On the eighth day the men's resistance to the cold began to lessen. The northerly Force 4 wind was freezing and the highest temperature was 34°F at midday. At nightfall several of the deckhands had no feeling left in their hands despite the protection of gutting gloves. But the cold wind seemed to revive Graham, and he was soon working at his normal speed, after being called at 0550 hours.

On the ninth day it was noticeable that Graham and the crew, especially those over forty, were eating less because of their fatigue. They could no longer face the huge meals they ate on arrival at the fishing grounds, and found it difficult to eat anything after their watch below, sleeping.

During these nine days, Graham averaged six hours sleep a day, and worked for an average of sixteen hours a day. At the end of this period he looked physically exhausted. His pupils were dilated, and his blank stare and unco-ordinated movements made him stagger at times like a drunken person. I suspect that he was at a low ebb mentally as well, because of the constant antagonism between himself and other crew members. He seemed equally upset and ready to argue when he was shown either kindness or harshness.

On the tenth day, catches were poor, and the crew managed to snatch a few hours extra sleep during the day. Graham worked for a total of thirteen-and-a-half hours on deck, in fine weather and good conditions.

Because of the poor catches, the ship steamed south for twelve hours at midnight to a new fishing area. The crew were able to sleep during this time, but most of them woke up with splitting headaches, due to the unaccustomed sleep, and with frayed tempers.

This led to one of the greasers going on strike because of an argument with the Chief Engineer, and two other crew members nearly had a fight at dinner. Graham was involved in two really bad arguments, and in the end he refused to work and went below to his bunk. He worked for five hours on that day.

Catches were better on the new grounds, and between midnight and 0700 hours on the 16th, the crew members on watch never left the deck, even for a mug of tea.

This was the last day on the fishing grounds, but the crew had to work harder and for longer periods than any previous day. The crew had to spend four hours in a chain-gang shovelling ice up from the hold to make room for the heavy catches. The Skipper persuaded Graham to go back to work at 0700 hours. The final haul was made at 2015 hours, but all crew members had to stay on deck until 0300 hours the following morning to clean up the deck, and secure the heavy and complicated fishing tackle.

Graham was twenty hours without sleep, and apart from two meal breaks, was engaged for nineteen hours on extremely heavy manual work. Other crew members spent twenty-seven hours on deck without sleep. Many looked exhausted, with pale, drawn faces and deep purple and black lines of tiredness under their eyes, but everyone was cheerful after 1800 hours on the 16th when the Skipper passed the word that we were going home after the next haul.

Homeward Voyage

2045 hours 0500 hours
Saturday, 16 April 1966 Wednesday, 20 April 1966

On the 17 April, after 0300 hours most of the deckhands slept all day, apart from a three hour spell on watch in the wheelhouse. Those who did get up for meals ate very little and hardly spoke at all. They appeared dazed with tiredness. Graham got up and ate a small tea, and went straight back to his bunk until 0700 hours the following morning.

During the remainder of the homeward voyage, he spent an average of eight hours a day repairing damaged nets and warps, and cleaning up the deck and interior of the ship. He was able to catch up on his sleep, but still looked pale and tired when the ship docked at Grimsby, by which time the rest of the crew had fully recovered.

Conclusions from the Voyage

1. Factors Causing Physical Fatigue

a) The long working hours – averaging 16–16½ hours when fishing.

b) The heavy manual work.

c) The lack of sleep, an average of 5½–6 hours a day.

2. Factors Helping to Combat Physical Fatigue

a) The large quantities of hot food cooked in iron containers.

b) The large quantities of tea and sugar consumed.

c) The reviving qualities of the cold rarefied air – *but* in winter, the cold which becomes intense is a factor causing fatigue.

d) Extremely good physiques, especially in the chest, back and arms.

3. Factors Causing Mental Strain

a) The monotonous, repetitive work.

b) Being confined aboard a small ship with twenty other men for three weeks at a time.

c) Worrying about families and loved ones at home.

d) The need to take the greatest precautions at all times when working amongst the dangerous deck machinery.

4. Factors Helping to Combat Mental Strain

a) Looking forward to the next meal, the next tot of rum, and the next watch below.

b) Good crew morale and friendliness.

c) The crates of beer and spirits in the ship's bond.

d) Smoking: *but* between 1948 and 1964, 229 trawlermen died at sea from disease and the latest figures.[1] show a particularly high incidence of malignant growths in general, and cancer of the stomach in particular. Excessive mortality from cancer of the respiratory tract was also found. This is not surprising in view of the excessive numbers of cigarettes smoked by trawlermen.

e) Continuous use of obscene language.

Notes

1. In 1966

Ice Top-Hamper

'IN ADDITION TO THE HAZARD of black ice, there is the danger of ice on ships operating in low air temperatures. Particularly vulnerable are the distant-water Arctic trawlers operating in the Greenland and Barents Seas. The problem is ice top-hamper caused by freezing spray when the air temperature is less than −2°c. 'Green' water will not freeze readily unless trapped by choked scuppers[1] and at very low temperatures (below zero Fahrenheit) spray will consist of ice crystals and will not adhere.

'Recent design of such ships has attempted to eliminate, as far as possible, the top-hamper on which the spray can freeze and a tripod foremast has been found much more preferable to the normal foremast with standing rigging. The danger has been illustrated by the fact that on a seven hundred ton trawler over a hundred tons of ice can form with a centre of gravity *thirty feet above the level of the deck.*'[2]

The aftermast carrying the sail and standing rigging was also eliminated but ships were still lost. It is possible that some of the distant-water vessels, 'lost without trace', capsized from ice top-hamper. Others were known, all occurring north and east of Iceland, where there is a large area of open sea and no chance of shelter.

On the 23 January 1955 most trawlers in the vicinity of Iceland were sheltering from severe weather conditions at Ritur Huk.

The *Roderigo* (formerly the *Princess Elizabeth*) was steaming in close company with the *Lorenzo*[3] whose radar had become faulty. They had gone to the aid of the *Kingston Garnet*, caught in severe weather conditions, with a fouled propeller. However, the *Kingston Garnet* managed to clear the screw and reach shelter, but the *Roderigo* and *Lorenzo* were now in danger from the severe gale force winds and freezing weather conditions.

For three days, the two trawlers fought the atrocious weather. Had they tried to go about they would have capsized. Unable to turn and run for shelter, they had to face up into the wind and frozen spray. The build up of ice top-hamper was inevitable. On 26 January, ninety miles east of North Cape, Iceland, they were finally overwhelmed by the continual build up of ice.

Some trawler crews claimed to have heard the last messages from the two ships just before they capsized, but a radio expert I spoke to said that with thick ice on wires and aerials it would have not been possible to transmit radio messages. Whichever is correct, forty men lost their lives going to the aid of others in distress.

We discussed this tragedy on the *Oratava*. I mentioned the steam hoses used by the Royal Navy on Arctic Convoys in World War II to clear their guns of ice. For once 'Elvis' was very patient with me, 'Look, you don't understand. They was so badly froze up they couldn't get out on the fuckin' deck.' I remember it was very quiet for the rest of that mealtime.

In January 1968, within the space of ten days, three more Hull trawlers were lost through ice top-hamper. In severe weather conditions, trawlers fishing the north-west coast area of Iceland had run for shelter, some to Breidafjord and other including the *Ross Cleveland* into Isafjord. Trawlermen who were in that area at the time described the weather as 'atrocious', 'freezing very hard' and 'blowing very hard'.

Within the comparative shelter of the fjord the ice covered *Ross Cleveland* suddenly capsized. As the trawler went over, the mate who had been working on deck managed to launch an inflatable covered life raft. He jumped into the life raft followed by one of the firemen and the galley boy. For two hours they drifted to the end of the fjord where the raft beached. During that time the fireman and the galley boy died in the severe cold. The mate survived because he was wearing fully protective clothing.

In a blizzard the mate began walking blindly until he bumped into an obstacle which afforded him some shelter from the wind. A few hours later a farmer found him almost frozen to the door of his barn. The mate survived because of his fitness and the protective clothing, only losing four toes from each foot from frostbite. He swore he would never go back to sea again, yet six months later he sailed again as a skipper.

He was the sole survivor of the crews of three trawlers. Of the other two, the *Kingston Peridot* seems to have capsized at a placed call Melrakka Flats, east of Iceland, her radio communications growing fainter and fainter with the build-up of ice. All they found of her was an oil slick. The third trawler, *St Romanus* was last seen heading north, north-east from North Cape, Iceland. She did not have a radio operator aboard at the time and disappeared 'without trace'.

With the loss of these three vessels, questions were at last raised in Parliament concerning the safety of British trawlermen and the stability of Distant Water vessels. This led to the 1969 Holland-Martin Report revealing to the world just how dangerous fishing was, particularly in distant water, and also a campaign on safety.

In 1968 a support ship, the *Miranda*, was sent to northern waters. One of her tasks was to attempt to provide an accurate weather forecast for distant-water trawlers.

A month after the loss of the three ships, the *Boston Phantom*, was selected to take part in de-icing tests. Rubber tubes, 15ft long were fitted to the mainstay of the foremast. Compressed air was then pumped in and out of the rubber tubes, cracking ice as it formed, as the tubes inflated and deflated. Later that year *Boston Phantom* was fishing off Iceland on full-scale trials of the new de-icing equipment.

In January 1969 as the tests continued off Iceland, the weather deteriorated and a three-hour period of intensive icing occurred. *Boston Phantom*'s equipment worked so well that she was the only trawler able to remain fishing safely.

It was pointed out that the de-icing equipment was not designed with the intention of forcing vessels to remain at sea in dangerous sub-zero temperatures, but to give the ships time to run for shelter safely. The de-icing equipment had been tested and proven, but there is no record of it ever being installed and used on another trawler.

As late as 1978, the problem of ice top-hamper was still being considered. In Appendix 1 of the *Department of Trade Recommended Code of Safety for Fishermen*,[4] entitled 'Reducing the adverse effects of ice accretion upon the vessel's stability' the following recommendations were made:

1. Skippers should consider the implications of sailing into areas and weather conditions where there is a risk of icing up.

2. Ensure that they have adequate means for removing ice if required.

3. Allowances for added weight on a trawler's stability due to icing up do not mean that it is safe to continue fishing or remain in the area.

4. Under icing up conditions steps *must* be taken to begin *clearing the ice and moving to a warmer area* before the stability is reduced below the level considered adequate for reasonable safety.

Notes

1. Gaps along the sides of a ship, level with the deck which allow seawater which has come aboard to drain away and prevent flooding of the decks.
2. *The Polar World*, Patrick D. Baird (Longman's).
3. Sometimes referred to as the *Lorella*.
4. *Department of Trade Recommended Code of Safety for Fishermen* (HMSO 1978).

The Enigma of the Gaul

IN RECENT YEARS few ship losses have attracted as much attention as the loss of the Hull Stern Trawler *Gaul* which disappeared off North Norway in storm force weather conditions in mid-February 1974.

Built in 1972 by Brooke Marine Limited in Lowestoft for the Ranger Fishing Company and originally named *Ranger Castor*, she was considered to be a very 'safe' and 'seaworthy' vessel.

A Lowestoft teacher of my acquaintance was at the launching ceremony and had been shown all over the ship. She was visibly shocked by the loss and I remember what she said: 'But why didn't they call for help? They had three sets of radio equipment on that ship. I know, I saw it all.'

There were seventeen or eighteen ships in the area when the *Gaul* disappeared, and of them all, the *Gaul* was the most modern trawler and should have been the least likely to founder. But she had disappeared 'without trace'. There was no wreckage or visible sign of loss, not even a patch of oil. An extensive search was carried out by all ships in the area, including the Royal Navy, but nothing was found.

The first Court of Enquiry into the loss of the *Gaul* concluded that she must have been overwhelmed due to natural hazard, the wind and the sea. But there were nagging doubts in the minds of the relatives of the thirty-six crew members lost.

The matter might have ended there, but a few months later a lifebelt bearing the name *Gaul* was picked up off the North Norwegian

coast. Now matters took on a sinister note because the lifebelt was found to be a 'plant'. Prolonged forensic tests proved that it was one of the *Gaul*'s lifebelts, but the minute marine growth on it also proved that it could not have been floating about in the sea for several months. The algae was found to be freshwater not saltwater.

This caused an uproar in Hull. Now the nagging doubts became open accusations; that the *Gaul* had been used as a spy-ship for covert spying operations, that she had been sunk by the Russians, and that Russia had 'planted' the lifebelt as a cover up.

For a quarter of a century now the relatives of those lost on the *Gaul* have campaigned bitterly in an attempt to find out the truth. Subsequent Courts of Enquiry failed to reach a satisfactory verdict, reaching the same verdict each time, that the ship had been overwhelmed by the atrocious weather conditions.

Two Channel 4 TV documentaries claimed that almost all of the Hull distant-water fleet had been involved in covert spying operations at one time or another, from counting the number of Russian warships leaving their northern bases, photographing these ships, to actually carrying a naval officer with them on White Sea fishing trips.

In 1997 they found the wreck of the *Gaul* further to the east of where she was thought to have sunk. It was the evidence of a Norwegian fishing skipper who said he had sighted the *Gaul* the night she was lost, which led the searchers to the right area. In the underwater survey carried out in 1998 cameras revealed that the stern doors to the trawl net ramp were open, and subsequent tests have proved that her after or trawl deck could have been completely flooded. With her stern deck pressed down by tons of seawater, causing lack of stability, a large wave hitting the port side would have caused the ship to capsize. This swift and sudden end would explain why there was no distress call from the *Gaul*.

This explanation for the loss of the *Gaul* has generally been accepted, but I feel there are still questions that need answering.

Why, during her final days, was the ship involved in so much coming and going in the North Cape area? These were not the normal movements of a trawler searching for better catches of fish. It is almost as if they were searching or waiting for something.

Why were the stern doors to the fishing deck left open in the severe weather conditions?

Is it just coincidence that the wreck of the *Gaul* is lying near a 'SOSUS' cable, part of the system used by the Allies in the cold war to detect the movements of Russian submarines?

Why did the Norwegian skipper wait so many years before speaking about his sighting of the *Gaul*?

The most intriguing question remains: Who 'planted' the *Gaul*'s lifebelt and why?

The Saga of the Sargon

O F THE MANY TRAWLERS which were lost in Arctic waters,
disappeared 'without trace', two came home, long after all hope
had been given up for them. This is the story of one of them.

On 17 December 1921, the Grimsby steam trawler *Sargon* sailed for
a Christmas trip to the White Sea fishing grounds. At 110 foot long she
was a small ship for such distant waters. She had no radio, few trawlers
did in those days. She carried a crew of only ten men; trawlermen from
Aberdeen, Lowestoft, Hull and Grimsby.

In the narrow stretch of sea between the north of Scotland and southern
Norway they came across a disabled trawler and spent the next forty-eight
hours towing her into Aberdeen.[1]

Resuming her northern passage the *Sargon* ran into head winds and
heavy seas. Eventually they reached the shelter of the north Norwegian
fjords and steamed through them.

On Christmas Day the *Sargon* reached the White Sea off the North
Russian coast, where in 1921 there was only a three-mile territorial
waters limit. Catches for the next few days were only poor to moderate.
The skipper began to ease the *Sargon* in (where the catches were better)
and out of the three mile limit.

Luckily for the crew of the *Sargon* they had
just finished a trawl and had all the nets and
gear inboard, when

they spotted a Russian gunboat coming after them. The skipper decided to make a run for it. He rang down for full speed and told the chief engineer via the voice pipe to 'Give us all you've got'.

He did, but the gunboat was rapidly overhauling the small trawler, shuddering along as the chief engineer pushed the engines to their limits.

Then they had their second stroke of good luck. As they steamed north they encountered an ice field and the skipper took them into it. The captain of the gunboat decided not to risk following into the icefield and after firing a few shells at the *Sargon* turned and began steaming around the edge of the ice.

Their luck held. They made it safely through the ice and joined a large fleet of British trawlers. Several hours later, the gunboat re-appeared having steamed around the edge of the ice, but, unable to distinguish which trawler they had been chasing, the Russians turned away.

The *Sargon* resumed fishing and by the end of the first week in January, the fish room was full and they were ready to return home. But first they would have to put into North Norway as their fuel was running low. The tow, the bad weather and the high-speed chase had severely depleted their stocks of coal.

Unfortunately, the fuel they took on board was very poor quality coal from the mines up on Spitzbergen, and for the crew of the *Sargon* it was to prove almost fatal.

The *Sargon* at last began her homeward bound voyage. She had left the Norwegian coast when a ferocious storm blew up from the south-west. All they could do was hold the ship head to wind. The storm lasted for days during which time the *Sargon* could make no progress at all, despite the fact that the engines had to be run at full speed in order to keep the ship head to wind. If they had tried to turn the trawler and run for shelter off Norway, the ship would have heeled over and capsized in the atrocious weather conditions.

The poor quality Spitzbergen coal was burning at too fast a rate and when the storm finally died down there was very little left in the bunkers. The skipper decided that they would have to refuel in the Faroe Islands, but with fifty-seven miles still to go the coal ran out.

Their situation now called for desperate measures. Everything that could be burned was taken down to the engine room. Bunks were chopped out, mattresses and blankets burned. Every scrap of wood, rope, rags and paper that they could find went on the boiler, but when all this was used up, they were still a long way from the Faroes.

They made a sail out of tarpaulin and rigged it up on the foremast, and set the sail on the after mast. But in the end, the wind blew the jury rigged sail away. Their situation was now serious and their only hope was a passing ship, but their luck had finally run out.

Grey day followed grey day as the *Sargon* wallowed helplessly in the Arctic swells with only the after sail and a sea anchor to steady her. Grey skies and grey seas day after day with only a few gulls and mollymawks for company.

After the first week, the food ran out and they began to eat the fish they had caught, but by the end of the second week their mouths became so lacerated and ulcerated from the salt and iodine in the fish, they had to give up this, their only source of food. They also ran out of tea at the end of the second week. From now on their only drink would be water.

They managed to trap the occasional seagull and one account states that they had a final meal of rats and crumbs scraped out of the foodbins. They could not even rest comfortably. All they had was the deck to rest on. They had chopped up their bunks, burnt their mattresses, blankets and even burnt the coir matting covering the floors of their cabins in the desperate effort to keep up enough steam to reach the Faroes.

As the weeks passed they grew weaker each day from malnutrition. The ship was cold. The only semblance of warmth came from the gas carbide lamps they lit in the main cabin each night.

The fish in the hold began to stink and they began to move it up out of the fish hold and throw it over the side, much to the delight of the seabirds accompanying them. But after a time they grew too weak to manage even this work and the remaining fish had to be left to rot.

On the 3 March, the skipper wrote in the ship's log: 'If help does not come within the next two days, most or all of this ship's crew will be dead.'

In the early hours of the next morning they saw a light and as dawn came they saw that it was another trawler. They fired distress rockets and the German trawler quickly came to their aid. The crew of the foreign vessel were shocked by what they saw on the *Sargon*. They fed the men and took her in tow to Iceland, which lay just over the horizon.

During the six week drift they had been unable to ascertain their position by the sun or the stars because of the interminable overcast. They had drifted all the way across the Arctic Ocean from Norway to Iceland.

Back home in Grimsby the *Sargon* had long been posted overdue and then presumed lost. On 6 March the dependants of the crew gathered at the offices of the ship's owners for the meagre insurance payouts due to them.

But just before they began paying out the money, the miracle happened. A clerk rushed into the offices excitedly waving a telegram stating that the *Sargon* and her crew were safe.

It was two weeks later that the [ST] *Sargon*, [GY] 858 came steaming proudly up the Humber River, her crew lining the deck. Most of the relatives were waiting on the quayside of the North Wall and a large crowd was gathering to see the trawler that had 'come back from the dead'.

The emotional scenes that followed as the crew came ashore must have been just like those at Aintree when 'Rummy' won the Grand National for the third time. Tears of joy, wonder, and admiration, and an overwhelming sense of relief.

Notes

1. The owners of the *Sargon* would have been paid a good sum of salvage money for bringing the disabled trawler back to port, some of which should have been shared with the *Sargon*'s crew.

On Christmas Day in the Morning

THE SUCCESS OF A VOYAGE depended upon the relationship between the costs incurred and the receipts from the sale of the catch.[1] The latter depended on a combination of factors. The size, variety and quality composition of the catch, together with the levels of market prices prevailing at the time of the sale, were obviously important. Gross earnings for a vessel at the end of a voyage were dependent on sales at or above the general reserve prices applied at the port fish auction on the day of landing.

What a catch earned was also dependent on supply and demand. A surplus of fish on a particular day with trawlers landing large catches could have meant lower prices and less profit. Alternatively, a trawler landing a poor catch on a day of shortage would make more profit than expected.

Fluctuating markets were one reason why distant-water vessels fished all year round and Christmas time was no exception.

Kelly recounted the *Oratava*'s 1965 Christmas trip, under the command of an Icelandic relief skipper, (which upset the crew at the start of the voyage). They sailed out of the Humber on 18 December into a northerly gale, which did not abate. It took them six days to reach the shelter of the North Norwegian Fjords, which they passed through on Christmas Eve.

They reached their fishing position in the White Sea in the early hours of Christmas Day. At five o'clock the skipper gave the order to shoot the trawl, but it was bitterly cold and everything was so badly iced up on the foredeck that it took seven hours to free all the fishing gear. They finally got the net over the side at midday. 'At least we had a couple of hours to eat our Christmas Dinner.'

I asked Kelly if they got paid any extra money for being at sea over Christmas. 'Depends on the catch, but yer can usually earn double, sometimes treble what yer get normally, otherwise it's not worth comin'. I 'aven't 'ad a Christmas at 'ome for seven years now.'

Catches were moderate throughout the next week, and, at six o'clock on the evening of 31 December, the ship docked in Honisvag, the most northerly town in Norway for the traditional twelve hours ashore allowed to trawler crews, in order to celebrate New Year and as a perk for being at sea over Christmas. 'Six tomorrow morning,' warned the Icelandic skipper as the crew trooped ashore.

Liberal dosages of strong Norwegian aquavit ensured riotous New Year's Eve celebrations including several fights with the locals. Kelly could not remember much of what happened after midnight, or getting back to the *Oratava*, but he was back on time. Twenty-four hours later they were still in Honisvag, waiting for three of the crew who had gone adrift. I never did hear the end of this story or what happened to the three missing crewmen.

Sometimes trawlers who were short of crew members would pick up Norwegian fishermen in the fjords or from the northern towns. As these Norwegian fishermen preferred to be paid in fish there was no problem about sending them their wages.

Other Christmases were not so happy.

On Thursday 22 December 1966, the *Boston Welvale* ran aground at the base of cliffs on the shores of north-west Iceland in a Force 9 severe gale and blizzard. *Ross Renown* and *Prince Philip* stood by but were unable to close with the stranded vessel, or render any assistance because of rocks. All twenty-one of the crew were eventually hauled to safety up onto the top of the cliffs by Icelanders using breeches buoy apparatus. The story of how the *Boston Welvale* was eventually sold for £1 to a local Icelandic fisherman is told in *Boston Deep-Sea Fisheries* by Mark Stopper and Ray Maltby.

In the north Atlantic, three days later, in the early hours of Christmas Day, an explosion ripped through the engine room of the stern freezer trawler *St Finbarr*, crippling the ship. Ten of the crew were killed in the explosion and resulting fire. *St Finbarr*'s sister ship *Orsino* was soon on the scene and went alongside in heavy seas to render assistance. They got a towline aboard and then set about rescuing survivors. Thick black smoke was pouring from the hull of the burning trawler and in the high seas, one of *St Finbarr*'s crew was washed away and another died during the transfer.

Twelve die in Atlantic

CRIPPLED TRAWLER BLAZES AFTER EXPLOSION

Express Staff Reporters: FROM TORONTO, CANADA
FROM HULL, YORKSHIRE

Tuesday

THE 1,139-ton British trawler St. Finbarr, devastated by a Christmas morning explosion in the North Atlantic, was only a few miles from Newfoundland tonight, being towed by the trawler Orsino.

Twelve of the crew of 25 died. The 13 survivors and one body are aboard the Orsino which is making only three knots through 40 mile-an-hour winds and heavy seas.

Thick black smoke was still pouring from the hull of the burning St. Finbarr, an all-freeze trawler which

Sad tidings break up family parties—

ON CHRISTMAS DAY IN THE MORNING

For three days, unable to make more than three knots, the *Orsino* towed the stricken *St Finbarr* stern first through forty miles an hour winds, heavy seas and blizzards. With only forty miles to go to St Johns, Newfoundland, *St Finbarr* sank.

At the narrow entrance to St Johns, a Newfoundland pilot took over from the captain and a crowd began to gather on the quay as he brought the 1,500 ton *Orsino* round the headland. As the grey-hull trawler moved in amid a flurry of snow, to the surprise of the crew and *St Finbarr* survivors, the crowd on the quay began to applaud and cheer. The *Orsino*'s rescue duty had stretched across 800 miles of heavy seas, but to the crew it was just another day's work.

On the morning of Christmas Day, 1973, the skipper of the Hull trawler *Ian Fleming* decided to take the ship into the shelter of a Norwegian fjord, so that the crew could enjoy their Christmas dinner in calm water. But running into the fjord the trawler struck rocks killing three crewmen.

At the subsequent Department of Trade and Industry Inquiry in Hull, the deckhand in the wheelhouse with the skipper at the time of the accident claimed that he thought the skipper was steering the wrong way. He left the bridge to fetch someone of higher authority than himself, as he thought something was wrong, adding that as he was only a deckhand, he couldn't tell the skipper, 'You're going the wrong way.'

The skipper claimed that the steering had broken down. When the *Ian Fleming* continued turning towards the rocks, he stopped the engines and put them into reverse, but it was too late. The skipper also agreed that he should have taken on a local pilot.

The Marine Superintendent in charge of the inquiry found that no satisfactory conclusion could be reached because of 'conflicting statements'. A second inquiry also never reached a satisfactory conclusion, again, because of 'conflicting statements'.

This was the last serious incident involving a British Distant Water Trawler on a Christmas Day. There would not be many more to come.

Notes

1. In 1966 it cost £200 per day to keep the *Oratava* at sea in terms of fuel, wages, food and other sundries. For an average twenty-one day trip costs of £4,200 were incurred before any profit was made.

Cod Wars

'Port twenty.'
'Port twenty, sir.'
'Midships.'
'Midships, sir.'
'Hard a' starboard!'
'Hard a' starboard, sir.'
'Stop starboard, full ahead port.'
'Stop both!'
'Oh fuck it, leave it!'
CRASH!

AND YET ANOTHER Royal Navy Frigate was out manoeuvred and rammed by a small Icelandic Gunboat, simply because the latter vessel had a tighter turning circle.

In 1952 Iceland began extending her fishing limits, at first from three to four miles and then in 1958 to twelve. Since the fifteenth century, Icelandic waters had been traditional fishing grounds for Britain and other countries. But Iceland had become increasingly concerned about overfishing around her coasts because the fish were her main source of income.

Britain reacted to the twelve-mile limit by banning Icelandic vessels from landing their catches in United Kingdom ports. This first Cod War ended by agreement in 1961.

The second Cod War began in February 1973 when Iceland extended her exclusive fishing zone to fifty miles. This time confrontations between British trawlers and the Icelandic gunboats became violent when the gunboats began to cut the trawl warps, which was extremely dangerous. The recoil from the thick wire trawl warps, suddenly relieved of the weight of the net and gear, could have maimed or killed any trawlermen on deck. This was an additional worry for skippers who now had the added responsibility of keeping a lookout for gunboats and getting their men off the deck in time. The second Cod War ended in November

1973 with a temporary agreement allowing a restricted number of British vessels in, although in July 1974 the International Court of Justice ruled that Iceland was not entitled to exclude British and other foreign fishing vessels between the twelve and fifty mile limits.

In 1975, Iceland declared that from 15 October her fishing limits would extend to 200 miles. All foreign vessels were forbidden within the fifty mile zone and only limited permits were to be given for the two hundred mile zone. British trawlers ignored these restrictions and the third Cod War began. This time it was serious and for a time our trawlermen had to battle on alone.

For the second time Icelandic gunboats started harassing our trawlers and cutting their trawl warps. This time they opened fire on several vessels, but no British skipper was going to allow his ship to be stopped and boarded if he could help it. The Fleetwood trawler *Red Hackle* made a run for it when ordered to heave to. She came home with a shell hole in her bows near the waterline and her wheelhouse riddled with holes from machine gun bullets.

The skipper of the *Grimsby Town* turned at full speed towards the gunboat that had ordered him to steam into an Icelandic port, as if intending to ram. It was only after the gunboat fired a shell through the trawler's funnel that the skipper thought it was about time to surrender.

Newspaper reports at the time of the third Cod War described how the crews of some trawlers pelted the gunboat crews with fish as they came alongside, and I often wondered how they would fare at the hands of men like Kelly, Elvis and Young Tom.

Britain offered concessions, but could not accept the limitation of her catch to the very small tonnage demanded by Iceland. Talks broke down and many more incidents occurred on the fishing grounds. Four civilian vessels were sent up to assist the trawlers, but the men demanded Royal Naval protection and for the third time frigates were sent north. Relations between Britain and Iceland continued to deteriorate and on the fishing grounds dangerous encounters became more frequent. A gunboat rammed the *Viveria* midships while attempting to cut her warps; the frigate *Arethusa* was in collision with the *Odinn* while she was protecting the *Kingston Jade*, and the *Aldershot* was in collision simultaneously with the *Arsenal* and a gunboat. There were other frequent incidents of gear and ships being damaged, including most of the twenty-two Royal Navy frigates involved, and the Icelandic gunboats.

In February 1976, Iceland played her last card. She broke off diplomatic relations with Britain and demanded recognition of her 200 mile fishing limit or NATO would have to leave the strategic base at Keflavic. With the stability of NATO threatened, the British government succumbed to foreign pressures forcing the distant-water fleet to be withdrawn from Icelandic waters. This was the beginning of the end for distant water. When the rest of the world followed Iceland with 200 mile limits, there was nowhere left to go. Those that did try to continue fishing were harried as far north as Spitzbergen by gunboats until they too gave up.

A few distant water trawlers were converted to rig standby vessels, others were sold abroad, but the vast majority were scrapped. The owners were well compensated for the trawlers they had to lay-up, but the trawlermen got nothing.

Suddenly they were classified as 'casual' or 'part-time' workers not entitled to compensation or redundancy. It was an insult to skilled men who worked long hours often for three hundred days a year at sea. It was not until 1993 that some men were given small redundancy payments. Even then, unless a trawlerman had worked for one owner for two years, he was still considered a 'casual' worker and got nothing. Some of these men had worked on trawlers for over thirty years!

... And Other Wars

In times of war, in common with vessels of the Merchant Navy, trawlers were 'taken up, out of trade' to assist the Royal Navy. Part of the distant water trawlers' tasks was Convoy duty, their low sides making them ideal for picking men up out of the water. In 1942 the Hull trawler *Lord Middleton* was accompanying what was to become the worst convoy of World War II: [PQ] 17.

Just after midnight on 4 July 1942, in the daylight of the high Arctic summer, new ensigns were hoisted on board every American merchant ship which made up the majority of this outward-bound Russian convoy. Soon there would be nothing to celebrate on this particular Independence Day.

[PQ] 17 was one of the largest convoys sent to Russia, and one of the most heavily defended. As well as a large Royal Navy escort, to the north was a British Battle Fleet and to the north-west a powerful American Battle Fleet. The idea was that if the new German Battleship *Tirpitz* came out from her north Norwegian fjord base, the Allies could pounce on her and destroy her. The *Tirpitz* did sail, and the Norwegian Underground quickly got word through to the Admiralty two thousand miles away.

Decisions were made and orders were flashed through to the convoy that the escort commanders found hard to believe. The convoy was ordered to 'scatter' and the Royal Navy escorts were ordered to fall back to safeguard the heavy units of the British Battle Fleet.

The merchant ships scattered to all points of the compass and the slaughter began. E-boats, MTBs and destroyers sortied from their bases in northern Norway. The ever present U-boat packs closed in and the fighters and bombers took off from their airfields in north Norway, while the *Tirpitz* simply sailed back to her fjord base. All but three of the merchant ships comprising the convoy were sunk.

The captain of the *Lord Middleton* was a RNVR Lieutenant, a lawyer by profession. He used to spend his summer holidays as a supernumerary aboard distant-water trawlers fishing up at Spitzbergen. He reasoned that the further north they could travel, the more distance they could put between themselves and the enemy. *Lord Middleton*'s foc'sle two pounder and machine guns would have been of little use against what was coming at the scattered ships. Two merchant ships asked if they could accompany the trawler.

For the next forty-eight hours the distress calls were coming in – then, silence. *Lord Middleton* and the two freighters sailed north until they reached the edge of the Arctic ice, where they stopped to consider the best course of action. Reading through the cargo manifests they discovered that one of the freighters was carrying a large amount of white camouflage paint. There was enough to paint the starboard sides and superstructures of the three ships. They waited several days, painting the ships and waiting for the Germans to finish their search for any more lone ships of the convoy.

Then they moved slowly along the edge of the ice until they were in a position due north of the Kola Inlet, finally making a dash for Murmansk at their best speed, which they reached safely. One other freighter was led to safety by the Free Polish Navy ack-ack ship *Pozarica*, commanded by Captain Lawford, fighting off almost constant air attack until they reached the Kola inlet. Captain Lawford started off his own distant-water trawling company after the war. He was one of the few owners who was liked and respected by his men, because of his care and consideration of them and their families.

Even the Falklands Campaign saw trawlers in action. After swift conversions, their stern trawling gear changed for mine-sweeping equipment, the Hull distant water stern trawlers *Cordella*, *Furnella*, *Junella* and *Northella* of J. Marr Trawlers and *Pict* of United Trawlers sailed in company for the South Atlantic. The task of the *Pict*, which eight years earlier had searched in vain for her sister ship the *Gaul*, was to act as a tender for the other four.

South of Ascension Island, the five trawlers rode the long Atlantic swells and weathered the storms far more comfortably than other vessels, but this was the kind of weather they had been built to withstand. Manned by Royal Naval personnel, their official title was II Mine Countermeasure Squadron – MCM.

On the afternoon of 27 May 1982 at the old Whaling Station of

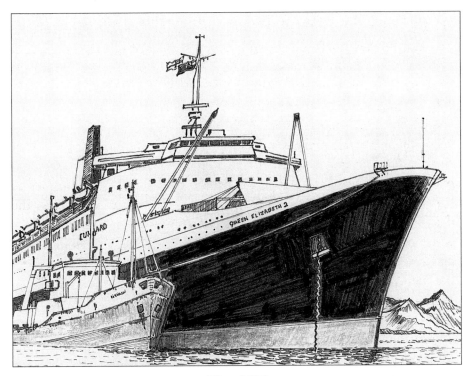

May 1982

Grytviken on South Georgia, the squadron began the transfer of the ill-fated 5 Brigade from the *QE2* to *Canberra*, and the Gurkhas from the *QE2* to the P&O Roll-on-Roll-off Ferry *Norland*. At the same time, they transferred casualties and survivors to the *QE2* from *Canberra* and *Norland*. The transhipping took over twenty-four hours.

After the Argentine surrender, the *Pict* was the first British ship to sail into Port Stanley on 15 June with *Junella* and *Cordella*, *Pict* began to sweep the outer harbour. *Northella* and *Farnella* arrived from South Georgia and by the beginning of July the two fields of moored mines had been cleared.

HMS *Junella* had the dubious task of taking a specimen mine back to Portsmouth for examination. Although the mine had been defused, it was still packed with high explosive on the 8,000-mile journey back to the United Kingdom. Sailing through the tropics they had to cover the mine with mattresses soaked in seawater, to protect it from the heat. Despite their dangerous tasks all five trawlers returned home unscathed.

Not so the Argentine trawler *Narwal*. This 2,500-ton factory ship was detected on 9 May by two Sea Harriers from HMS *Hermes*. The *Narwal* had already been warned off ten days previously. She was now back inside the Total Exclusion Zone and was behaving suspiciously. She was apparently acting as a spy-ship. She was ordered to heave to or accept engagement.

Either her crew were very brave or very foolhardy, or both, because the unarmed trawler did not react and continued westward at about 14 knots. The Sea Harriers attacked the *Narwal* with bombs (which failed to explode) and heavy cannon shells. She finally came to a stop with her engine room destroyed. Early reports of only one crewman injured later became twelve men killed, illustrating once again the vulnerability of this type of ship in wartime.

Much has been written about the Falklands War, but the trawlers are hardly mentioned. It is too easy to forget the vital part these vessels and their crews played in this and other wars, because of their unglamorous roles.

They are not forgotten. On the East Coast in a quiet park in North Lowestoft, there is a monument overlooking the sea. On it are the names of the hundreds of fishermen who did not make it back to port. Each October there is a memorial service and it's a moving experience to stand with an ever dwindling number of their shipmates by that monument. Perhaps, like me, they also reflect on what was once a great industry, and what a privilege it was to see it all at first hand.

It is now a quarter of a century since the demise of distant-water trawling and ex-trawlermen now realise just how risky and dangerous it all was. But given the calibre of these men, I feel that many of them, given the chance, would return to those icy northern wastes.

For my own part, I can only express my gratitude to Skipper James Nunn and the crew of the *Oratava* for getting a clumsy student home in one piece.

POSTSCRIPT: FEBRUARY 2001

On a winter holiday in the Gambia early this year I came across the wreck of the *Ross Revenge* [GY] 718, the largest 'sidewinder' ever based at a British port. On a day when the temperature had reached 100°, from a high vantage point in the seaport of Banjul, I spotted the high flared bow of a British distant water trawler, down by the stern, lying

out in the bay. An Arctic trawler for nineteen years, she became the home of Radio Caroline in 1983. Sold on a few years ago to become an offshore radio station off the West Coast of Africa, she now lies rotting in Banjul harbour, her flared bow, built to withstand the Arctic, pointing defiantly at the hot African sun. If I ever become a big lottery winner, I'll bring her home and restore her to the fine ship that she once was.